AF601809

ELVEA
Bücher & eBooks

Imprint

Published by Elvea
1st edition 2020
ISBN: 978-3946751366

Translated from German: Barbara Johann
Editing of the original version: by Harald Braem
Print: Uwe Köhl
Graphic layout: Barbara Baer
Cover illustration: Dimitris Kolyris

German 1st edition:
Die Macht der Farben

Die Macht der Farben. Bedeutung und Symbolik

Harald Braem

The Power of the Colours

Meaning & Symbolism

Contents

Preface

When the first edition of "The Power of The Colours" was published in Germany in 1985, the book was designed to be a working tool for my students at the University of Applied Sciences in Wiesbaden and it was tailored to the needs of the Departments of Communication, Design, Architecture and Interior Design. It was meant to be an easily understandable introduction into the interesting field of the then still new Science of Colour Psychology. More than twenty years of practical research and tests followed covering the areas Marketing, Public Relations and Advertising, Medicine, Psychology, Fashion, Sports, Politics, and Entertainment Industries together with the KULT-UR-INSTITUT for Interdisciplinary Research and in cooperation with my late friend and colleague Prof. Dr. Harald Brost (Institute for Light, Colour and Room). In the process we were able to confirm important results of the research by Johann Wolfgang von Goethe, Johannes Itten, Prof. Max Lüscher, Heinrich Frieling, Warden, Flynn and other colour researchers to an unexpected extent and prove these results scientifically.

"The Power of The Colours" affects all areas of private and social life and is subject to permanent control and updating by daily practical experience. For example, we all saw how the world was shaken by the attack of September 11th 2001 and we witnessed how the colour fashion in the free democratic world in West and East (!) changed from red to blue in the colouring choice of numerous products, most notably in the automobile industry. Apparently, the current emotion and awareness matrix of the mobile and global society is blue. Companies, whose Corporate Identity and Corporate Design was already designed in blue, experienced disproportionate increase of competence, boost of sales and profits, surpassing the average limits of growth. In many areas ranging from sports to TV news stations blue is seen as a warranty of faithfulness similar to the UN blue helmets and the blue uniform of the "Eurocops". Blue stands for quality of life, freedom and contentment and has become the favourite colour of all modern people from Tokyo to Berlin and New York. The secret seems to be the variety of hues. Each individual can find their own favourite blue.

Orange – the natural vivid, sparkling counterpart of the rather calm blue – has lived up to its role as a sensual and bodily oriented popular figure. Let's remember the Orange Revolution in the Ukraine – a laughing female rock singer with lots of sex appeal became the icon for the revolution. Or the German chancellor Angela Merkel who changed her image in the campaign and was elected in an orange costume. After the election Merkel returned to the usual strict, self distancing black which is the traditional colour choice of the conservative Christian clientele. So, orange can be used for sudden changes, at least temporarily. We see more and more orange flags waving all over the world, they have already become an international symbol for a peaceful paradigm shift. With orange things can be put in motion, you can change behaviour in a likeable way, but with blue you can rule for a long time because blue represents the longing for order, fidelity and reliability and a last resort.

Both colours seem to require each other. That is why in many sports they are an ideal combination of colours for winner type jerseys. Of course, it's not the colours but the performance of the team who decides if sports or politics are successful in the long run, the colours only underline the effort.

Wherever we look – ADS or Indigo children, the violet Milka cow (German chocolate commercial), Greenpeace, the Mediterranean design of the Pope's home, women power, colours of carpets, the yellow sunglasses of the hip smiley generation, jersey colours at the FIFA World Cup, the Tour de France or the new design of an office – the power of the colours is visibly acting everywhere under strict rules and with predictable regularity. And: the power can be used intentionally. To re-emphasize its role: "The Power of the Colours" was not written as a commentary to certain events, quite the opposite is true: events happened and proved the prior statements.

Unsurprisingly, national and international media took notice over the time and focused on specific phenomena of the colour psychology. The book became a long time bestseller, it was translated into many languages (most recently into Russian, Chinese and Korean) and was covered by many radio and televi-

sion features (Terra X, ZDF). It's high time that all the information about colour psychology is made available in the English-speaking areas.
At first you may be surprised about our decision to go without illustrations. But soon you will realise that in this case nice pictures are indeed unnecessary because the best pictures are always created in your own mind. This book invites you to an expedition and you are challenged to see new images, to identify ancient patterns and to realise unforeseen correlations. If this happens, I made my small contribution to widen our horizon.

Harald Braem
Nierstein 2020

The Power of the Colours

Whatever we do – when we decide on a new car or a new dress, when we shop in a supermarket or furnish our home, when we orient ourselves quickly in traffic situations or leisurely watch a photo book or when we choose a proper Christmas gift – we are always dealing with the secret power of the colours. Colours influence, check and control our whole thinking, feeling and acting in a very effective and lasting way. This happens even more when we pay the least attention.

Can we accept this statement? Aren't colours something very personal and subject to individual taste as well as fashion? Isn't it true that each person reacts to colour in a different way and depending on the situation?

Of course, the subjective sense plays an important role. Also the personal taste, appeal and rejection, imitative instinct and deliberate distance thereof, personal touch and fashion. But if we believe that this is covers the issue, we mix up cause and effect. We would only discuss the surface and manifestations and thus we only scratch the surface of a phenomenon which has much more depth and roots back into the olden times of humankind.

We call such characteristics "archetypical", we could also speak of "ancestral imprints". A lot of research

about this issue has been done in the field of depth psychology (mainly by C.C. Jung) which unearthed some astonishing connections. When we are born we do not start from scratch as a "blank sheet" waiting to be "written on" by society and environment. No, inside of us, in the genetic code of our cells and in the old centres of our brain, we carry relics of the collective memory of the whole mankind which shows in behaviour patterns and reflexes, in structures of our thinking, in images and dreams.
The colours are such ancestral imprints, too. More precisely: the feelings that had been once identified with a colour and the qualities of cultural impression which have been allocated to the colours in the course of time.
For those who think that this sounds all very theoretical, I want to present a few examples which will immediately explain what we are talking about and will show how the effect of the colours is interwoven with biological-chemical-physical and psychic-mental processes in our body.

Example 1: The Matchbox Test

Make sure that nobody watches when you prepare the matchbox for the test as follows: empty the box and write the words hammer, violin/guitar, red on the inside of the box. Put the matches back into the box to give it the right weight and make it rattle in the usual way. Tell the test person that "this test is meant to test the concentration and skilfulness is of vital importance."

Take the matchbox between thumb and index finger of your left hand, perform a rotational movement with your hand and take over the box with the thumb and index finger of your right hand. Each time you rotate and take over the box count out loud the rotation.

That looks very simple and actually, it is simple. But you tell your test partner that you do not believe that he is able to rotate the box smoothly and regularly and keep counting out loud.

Of course, your test partner will disagree. Let him demonstrate how he can do it. Lo and behold – it works. Now you tell him the following: "Okay, that works fine for now. But I doubt that you are really able to focus. I am going to ask you a couple of questions you should answer spontaneously without thinking twice. They are no real questions, I just toss a catchword at you and you answer just as quickly with a word that comes to your mind. You will see how soon you forget about rotating and counting."

Now the test person will protest and will try hard to prove his ability to keep focussed. Let him count to six or seven and then ask very suddenly. "tool"? In almost 90% of all cases the test person will answer "hammer". Sometimes, in very few cases, the answer will be "pliers". Let the test person continue to rotate. When the counting comes to twelve or thirteen you ask "musical instrument?"

Again the answer will come spontaneously "violin" For younger test persons the answer may be "guitar", though. In the 60s and early 70s we could expect 90% of the answers to be violin. Over the years this changed, so that today 60% of the answers is violin and about 40% guitar. Other instruments are named only very rarely and only if the test person plays that instrument or if it is very important for him for some other reason.

The answer to the third sudden question “colour?”, which should be asked when the person is counting twenty or twenty one, is mostly “red” (about 80%) or sometimes “blue” (about 20%). Other colours are almost never chosen.

Thank the test person for taking the test, take the match box, throw out the matches and let the test person read out the prewritten result. People will be perplexed by this test, the surprise effect is on your side.

What happened in the test?

It’s very simple: The busier people are dealing with external things (here: focussing on rotating and counting), the less they are able to control the sub-conscious. “Archetypical” concepts emerge from the primordial pool of feelings, symbols and images which is the subconscious. The answers in the test are not reflected but they are readily available, re-callable programmes like instincts. Since the hand axe was invented the hammer always was the Number 1 tool and is closely connected with the history of mankind. Violin and guitar are (at least in our culture) the most popular instruments and Red is the oldest colour.

The oldest colour? What is that supposed to mean? Did not all colours exist from the beginning? At this point we do not answer this question. We will elaborate in the chapter "The Colour Red".

Example 2: The Heart

Give any random test person a selection of coloured crayons, felt tip pens or paints and ask them to paint a heart. It will always be a red heart, never a blue, yellow or green one.
Red hearts are common, we are used to them? Correct. But please carry out the same test with infants who have never seen anything about anatomy, transplantation, heart medication or love symbols. Without hesitating for a second they will pick the red colour. Of course, this is no "primordial knowledge". Their mothers or fathers once showed it to them. But one glance was enough to rediscover the "primordial programme". This always reminds me of the kittens whose mother house-trains them in virtually no time by setting a drastic example. One "demonstration" is enough to implement the primordial programme of all cats.

Example 3: The Strange Cases

A carrier in the USA was surprised about the fact that on some days his workers complained more and became exhausted much earlier than on other days. When he looked into the matter, he found out that on these days the workers had to carry dark cases, exclusively. Astoundingly, the weight of the cases was

identical with the weight of lighter coloured cases which had to be carried on other days.
Hallucination, Autosuggestion?
The American psychologists Warden and Flynn studied this phenomenon and had people estimate the weight of cases which had the same weight but different colours.
Instead of using relatively well known and "learnable" measures (i.e. one pound or one kilo) they used an "abstract" and irreproducible unit, a three- pound case.
The result sounds incredible: each colour weighs differently.

The result:

White (as default value)	3.0 pounds
Yellow (estimated)	3.5 pounds
Green	4.1 pounds
Blue	4.7 pounds
Grey	4.8 pounds
Red	4.9 pounds
Black (almost duplicated)	5.8 pounds

It's obvious that these results could not remain a secret and were not meant to remain a secret – quite the contrary: the industry picked up the idea enthusiastically and used it successfully – the simple choice of the right colour saves them all the common tricks like double bottoms and deceptive packages whose blown up the volume is designed to conceal the lack of content. A dark package of the same size and weight as a lighter coloured package gives an impression of being more compact, more concentrated, more massive and as such more valuable.

These days, every graphic and design student learns at an early stage how a purposeful colouring can manipulate not only weight but also taste, smell, consistency, quality, shelf life and freshness etc. They also learn how a combination of the right colours can change things, e.g. can turn big into smaller, heavy into lighter, bitter into sweet etc.

Are colours hidden persuaders?

They are much more than that! Colours do have a direct and massive impact on biochemical and biophysical processes in the human body which is largely uncontrolled by logical thought and reasoning. Hence colours influence the heart beat, pulse and breathing rate, they lower or raise the blood pressure, let wounds heal faster or slower, generate heat, coldness, hunger, thirst, ease, anxiety and aggression.
Nowadays most physicians and hospitals know about these things and take them into account in therapies. Designers, architects and interior designers have to consider such basic facts.
The following comparison of the colours red and blue shows the different influence the two colours have on the human body in order to illustrate what has been said.

Example 4: The Red-Blue Contrast

Red	***Blue***
breathing faster	breathing slower
pulse quickens and	pulse slows down and
blood pressure rises	blood pressure falls
heart beat sped up	heart beat slowed

All in all these facts mean: the sight of red colour excites and activates body functions while blue calms them down. This phenomenon becomes even more evident in tests to measure the individual sensation of cold and heat. The perception of cold and warm varies up to 13 °C.

Example 5: Sensation of Cold and Heat

In a room which is painted with teal colours people already sense cold at 15 °C while in a room with orange colours coldness is only perceived at 2 °C. A completely new aspect in the field of energy saving! All joking aside, popular sayings reflect clearly and strikingly that people are aware of these facts and backgrounds. Ice is commonly used as a synonym for blue and fire for red. Words like ice-blue and blazing red make it very evident and almost let us feel it physically which features man always allocated to the colours.

Let us sum up:
Talking about colours and the effect of colours is not a matter of taste which is open to discussion

although on the surface it seems to be just that for each individual case. In fact, colours are "visualized feelings" ("visualisierte Gefühle" according to Prof. Max Lüscher, the inventor of the well known Lüscher Colour Test). Even more: colours are intimately connected with archetypical, i.e. prehistoric experiences of mankind and cause clearly perceivable and measurable conditions.

The extremely important role colours play as a signal, design element, behaviour control element and manipulation element becomes evident when we remember that about 80% of all information are visual. The world is not just colourful – it uses the colours to organise and control its own meaning for man.

This book, which is deliberately not designed to be another textbook for chromatics, will not focus on theory but rather on discernible and "sensible" practice. As a popular scientific storybook the book resorts to the amateur wanting to make the "secret power of the colours" transparent for him. Therefore, instead of discussing complicated physical issues we will venture a look behind the curtains of the psyche. We will make an effort to approach prehistoric "primordial situations" in order to find out why people responded to different colours in the same particular way that is basically unchanged today.

In this book we will address cultural situations as well as historical events which caused fashion (i.e. deliberate imitation). We will also take a look at the vernacular language which functions like a seismograph in many respects.

Associations will be permitted as well as contradictions because to me nothing seems to be more restricting and detrimental for the expansion of consciousness than streamlined fundamental laws that have to be believed or – even worse – have to be learnt by heart.

No – life and gaining experience are flowing processes where detours and digressions should not only be useful but explicitly desired. If we want results which are mature and evolved over time, we should look at the most possible facets and aspects of a matter from all possible different angles.

After all, if science is supposed to be colourful and conspicuous, we need a fair amount of fantasy and the willingness to be fascinated or else science will be just grey theory as the proverb says (Grau, teurer Freund, ist alle Theorie – Goethe: Faust, line 2038)

But we are dealing with a "colourful" science in the literal sense. This science is very much alive for us because we are dealing with it at every turn in our normal course of life.

If this book helps to sharpen the view for colours and to make us more sensitive and more aware of the significance of colours, it will have achieved its aim.

On this note I wish you a lot of curiosity and fun and may you find some useful information in this collection of evidence in the case of colours.

It is a matter of personal taste - but how personal is our taste?

The first response of most people who hear about the psychology of colours for the first time is: "this is all very interesting but it does not apply to me, I have my own personal taste." Such replies sound awkwardly like the stereotypical statements we are told all the time: "This may be true for the masses but I am an individualist and my mind works in a very different way."

Or: "it's the masses who respond to advertisement but not me."

It's interesting to see how overestimation of one's own capabilities underlies such statements. Apparently people think of themselves as a unique, completely self-contained individual who is totally autonomous and resistant against any influence – quite in contrast to the manipulated masses. Individuality is "in", the masses are looked down upon, and they display the kind of uncritical behaviour the individualist does not want to be identified with.

However, since most people think that way we are dealing with a multitude of people who all think they are individualists and agree on this assessment galore thus generating a mass, after all.

Of course a personal taste does exist but we can safely assume that our taste is not unique in the world but it coincides with the "personal" taste of a multitude of other people much more often than we care to admit in our quest for individuality.

Tests and extensive polls show clearly reveal this misconception and put the myth "personal taste" into perspective showing that it's in fact the taste of a specific social group.

Also we have to ask what this so called "personal taste" is supposed to be. When we analyze its origin we will soon find out that personal taste is a hybrid evolving from a variety of already existing factors and imprints and is only mistaken for individualism.

The "normal" person is unaware of these factors. Let us analyze the "personal taste" systematically:

First of all there is fashion, the social taste or, rather: the social orientation of specific clearly identifiable interest groups in the society. The "personal taste" develops through interaction with this social taste by approving or rejecting what others are doing. Very often the "personal" aspect is already reduced to a mixture of various elements from various fashion styles.

But how does fashion come about? Fashion also does not fall from the sky but is a continuation, rejection or renewal of previously existing social taste and its hybrid forms.

Each fashion is based upon a certain conscious or unconscious symbolism which has formed over the time in a quasi historic process. Much of this symbolism, mainly the origin and history of particular

symbols lies in the dark for us today, maybe it emanates from the collective subconscious, the mysterious reservoir of all the archaic fears and dreams of mankind as well as fairy tales, legends and myths.
We can assume that all the concepts and sensations in the collective subconscious stem from primordial experiences.
Such primordial experiences are called primordial engrams, primordial impressions or archetypical situations. If you want to go back to their roots it's not enough to have knowledge of history, social science and psychology, you also need a considerable psycho-historical intuition.
When we find the origin we realise that we do not embody something new but we are simply the latest link in a chain that has been beaded through millions of years.
With regard to colours and their effect on human beings we come across other facts that disenchant the magic formula "personal taste" – namely the physiological conditionality, that is to say physical reactions which are caused by the biological compound of a human being and have precious little to do with individual opinion or taste. We will address the physiological effect of the colours in each chapter and take a closer look at the medical aspect of the physiological effect in the chapter "Healing with Colours".
In a nutshell we can say that colours are in fact – as Lüscher calls it – "visualized emotions" or to put it more profane: stimulus perceptions of the nervous system which have a pleasant or unpleasant effects depending on the disposition of the individual. Col-

ours are like resonance forces which prompts people to "resonate". The ability to "resonate", the extent to which this ability to resonate is favoured or inhibited or even blocked – that is how people actually differ from each other in principle, this is how their emotional state and in the end even their illnesses manifest themselves.
To close this chapter let me add a comment to rehabilitate the term "personal taste": when we take all these factors like fashion (social taste), symbolism, collective subconscious, archetypical imprint and physiological conditionality into account, only one erratic aspect is left to be considered: the individual subconscious.
The individual subconscious may well be based upon a primordial engram, an early imprint which is hidden deeply and unbeknown in the infancy of the individual person just like the archetypical situation is buried in the history of mankind. Only a depth psychological therapy can shed some light on possible influential experiences that cause profound changes in later life.
An example: We can say that blue is a colour which represents coldness, tranquillisation and longing in all aforementioned areas (social taste, symbolism, collective subconscious, archetypes, and psychological conditionality). But now we have a person who was scalded with hot water when s/he tipped over a blue cauldron. It is safe to assume that this person will not associate coldness with blue in later life (even though subconsciously) and will not long to be near something blue but will on the contrary – be

highly alarmed when coming close to blue items.
This is a severe disruption of the “normal” experience and in contrast to all other areas. Only such personal experiences stored in the individual subconscious, unusual connections which are either negating or extremely affirmative can profoundly influence the personality in a striking way.
Other than that “personal taste” is a blend of given basic elements, whereby the individual ego adds only small variations when putting the pieces of the puzzle together.
Let us not settle for a glimpse on the finished puzzle, let us take a closer look at the individual pieces. It’s not the outer appearance which epitomizes reality; the true character of reality always shows in the depth.

The Colours

The Colour Red

As far as we know red is in fact the oldest colour of mankind. How do we come to this conclusion?

First of all, we have linguistic research. In many countries annual "charts" of the hundred (or more) most used words of a language are published. With these charts changes of a language can be observed, we can see which words are standard usage, which words are fashionable or obsolete, and which consciousness has the strongest influence on the language.

For example, in the Federal Republic of Germany the "chart" reflects clearly that we are still living in an age of patriarchy: the words he, man, his and Mister are high on the list of frequent use while the equivalent female terms she, woman, her, lady etc are placed conspicuously farther down the list. Language is a give away.

It is also striking that red is the only colour listed among the first 100 words (even higher than position 20). All other colours, green, yellow, blue etc are either far down the list after position 100 or not on the list at all. Since such charts have been compiled red has always reigned supreme – not only here but in many countries and languages around the globe.

In fact, red seems to be – like the philosopher Hegel once said – "the tangible colour par excellence".

Looking closer into the matter and getting more involved into linguistic research (etymology: the studies of the derivation of words, research of language roots) we find that in fact red seems to be the oldest name of a colour in most languages of the world. In some languages, for example Russian, the name for "red" (krassni) is even identical with the name for "beautiful"

Obviously, red must have impressed people from the beginning. But what is it that makes red so unique, so fascinating and important? What must have happened when a colour is so indelibly ingrained into our subconscious?

Let us try to re-live such an influential primordial experience. Let us fall back for a couple of millenniums or even a million years into the dawn of human history:

Imagine that cavemen hunters have cornered a prehistoric buffalo. Blood is streaming from various arrow and lance wounds. The buffalo is irritated and ready for anything. One of the hunters is unwary, comes too close and is caught by the sharp horns and ripped up lengthwise. The man lies on the ground moaning and pressing his hands on the wound in a futile attempt to contain the plethora of his blood. In vain – from minute to minute his vitality is waning.

Finally, when the buffalo falls from several daring thrusts of the lance, the injured man has also taken his terminal breath. Covered in sweat and panting, waking up from hunting mode and a state of trance and ecstasy the men stand around. They see their companion lying motionless in a pool of blood. His lifeblood has drained away.

Red – the colour of life?

"Blood-red" or "Sanguine" is a very common name for red. And in Goethe's Faust Mephisto lets Faust sign the contract with his blood: "blood is a juice of rarest quality …"

We know that. We are civilised, we do not want to see blood. Many people already faint when they see a drop of blood for a blood test. That is a result of the culture barrier: blood must not be shed. To shed blood is a sin. However, this acquired behaviour does not seem to be very distinct. Usually, we do respond to the signal "red" correctly (for example a red traffic light). At least until we "see red". Under extreme conditions the "cultural barrier" breaks down very quickly. Just think about war, amok run, vendetta, and blood thirst – just remember bull fights and cock fights, ritual slaughtering and ritual sacrifices, religious self mutilation, Voodoo and Macumba.

But then it's not even necessary to relate to examples from the far and exotic. In our own environment it happens almost every day: when a lurid mass of onlookers runs together in a greedy wish to stare at bleeding victims of car accidents or when tens of thousands of people feel this inexplicable fascination watching sanguinary horror movies. Current favourites for teenagers (as a trial of courage) are video tapes with cannibalistic content.

The meaning of "actual" cannibalism was to incorporate the power and strength of the enemy together with his flesh and blood. Christianity continues this idea in the symbolic act of the Lord's Supper. "Eating" the body (wafer) and drinking the blood (wine) of the Lord is supposed to strengthen the faith of the believer. His blood was shed because it has the strength to make up for the sins of men.

However, blood is only one aspect (when we think of the colour red). Let us dive back into the olden days. Which element is it that has always magically attracted men because on the one side it consumes and destroys without mercy and on the other side it provides for food, on the one side it burns and on the other side it warms and protects – in short: it changes everything? It's of course the fire.

Nowadays we know that the ability to light a fire, to tame it and to use it deliberately caused a (maybe the most important) cultural impulse for mankind. It's easy for us to understand: raw meat was superseded by roast, a cold, unsociable cave was turned into a comfortable home and the darkness of the dangerous night was brightened like daylight by means of fire.

There were also the mysterious changes caused by fire. When ochre powder is heated the bright yellow brownish colour becomes crimson, the colour of blood. We all have watched the process when bricks are burnt. Therefore people in the early Stone Age regarded burnt ochre as a sacred colour and used it to mark certain spots on the game which they painted on the cave walls as part of magical incantation rituals (Altamira, Lascaux etc)

Fire has always tremendously appealed to people and still does today. Haven't we all at some point been sitting by a fireside or a campfire staring into the dancing lambent flames magnetised and fascinated? How easily the cultural barrier can be vaulted in case of fire is shown by pyromaniacs playing with fire. These "firebugs" become arsonists due to a morbid passion.

Fire is power; it is unleashed and destructive passion. If you ever watched the rage and violence of a furious forest fire you will never forget this experience.

Is red the colour of fire, then?

No, it's not only the colour of fire. An old proverb reveals that there is a third component beside fire and blood. It says,

Love is red and blood is red,
Red is the devil in his rage.

Is red also the colour of love?

Yes, but surely not love in a calm and platonic form. We are talking about the physical aspect of love, about sex and sensuality. Not a stealthily smouldering fire but aroused embers being fully ablaze.

We already spoke about the red heart as the simplest symbol of love in the previous chapter. There is a theory about the origin of the shape of the heart. The theory says that the nude bottoms of women who crawled into the cave in front of their men served as a model for the shape of the heart. It's quite a crude reference but gives us an idea how closely the heart symbol is connected with sex and eroticism.

By he way, could you imagine "certain quarters" with blue or green lights? No, the red lights of the

establishments speak for themselves; they do not require further explanation.
Let us wrap up: red stands for experience with the primordial encounters with blood, fire and love.
Before we take a closer look at the colour red from the perspective of depth psychology, let us take you on a journey through the ancient times and more recent history which will highlight more facets of the characteristics and peculiarities of the colour.
Red was already a precious colour in Egypt where the daughters of the Pharaoh used it to enhance their beauty as is well documented. In those days it became fashionable to paint cheeks, lips and fingernails. But what an exorbitant price had to be paid for this: in order to get tiny amounts of the precious crimson paint, slaves had to collect thousands of purple murexes, mash them and boil them to a brew. The red colour of the snail comes from a small (sex hormone) gland.
In ancient Rome the flashy colour was also very popular. However, only very few rich people could afford the expensive colour. Initially, only members of the Senate were allowed to wear red togas, later they became popular in the wealthy society circles.
There was a guild only for the production for the colour which was subject to strict supervision by the government and was bound to keep all professional secrets. Considering the fact that over ten thousand purple murexes were needed to extract a mere gram and considering that the dying of one kilogram of wool cost an equivalent of 4400 $ makes you realise how precious and luxurious the purple colour was.

After a real boom of the purple dyeing brought various cities like for example Tarent wealth and prestige, the formula to make colour from the purple murex gradually fell into oblivion.
The Byzantium emperors still signed their letters with purple red ink (today we only know the red ink our teachers use to correct mistakes).
After the fall of the Roman Empire the use of purple went out of fashion completely. Only much later Red was widely used when it was gained from the madder root (called Old Red or Persian Red, today it is synthesized and known as carmine).
For a long time red was a clear sign of power and violence. Executioners wore the red robe, cardinals and kings wore the red coat as a sign that they were masters of life and death.
Red was also the colour of Mars, the Roman war god. The red flag, the so called "flag of blood" was used in the Roman army for the first time. Running up the flag signalled the imminent attack: blood would be shed.
Later, in the French Revolution, countless red flags symbolized the violent coup d'état. And this has been that way up to this very day. It's hard to imagine a sea of blue, green or multi colour flags. However, red banners fluttering in the wind look like lambent flames, they provoke people and generate a collective feeling of violence and determination.
We find the colour red as a symbol of seizure manifested in many crests and flags. Looking at 97 countries, 77 out of the 97 flags contain the red (according to W. Köhler). Red is even the main colour of 21

flags. This does not mean that all these states are revolutionary, much rather the red colour is used as the colour of the united population.
We know the effect of red on big crowds. Just think about bull fights and football teams wearing red jerseys signalling extraordinary fighting strength, activity and dynamic. In both examples it's the audiences who are attracted, stimulated and agitated.
Apparently, there is a strong interaction between audience and players. "Red provokes applause. Due to the subliminal effect of the colour the fan in the stadium soon makes up his mind: this is the stronger team. They are winners. As a result the red team is applauded for minor success even in an away match. The benevolence of the audience then encourages the players and stimulates them to give maximum performance which in return will be rewarded with more applause. As a result the team has almost the same advantage as playing a home match." (Lüscher)
Goethe (who was not only a poet but also a scientist who researched colours empirically) describes the impression of red in his "Theory of Colours" as follows: "The effect of this colour is as unique as its nature. The active part is of highest energy here and it's no surprise that energetic, healthy and crude people in particular enjoy this colour." This already says a lot about the character of the colour.
The influence of the colour red on men always was and still is as multi faced and as "loud" as life itself:
In ancient China Red was the lucky colour which drove away diseases and evil spirits, it was also the

colour of wealth. Up to this day a red faced man in Chinese theatre represents a holy person.

Redheaded people, on the other hand, suffered in my cultures: in Egypt they were held responsible if fields were barren and they were killed. In the Christian Occident (maybe except for Ireland) red headed women were regarded as the wantons of the devil who had "marked them with his hellish colour". In the Orient, on the other hand, and in India many people dye their hair red with henna to fit the beauty ideal.

Many Indian tribes used red colour to conjure demons. For the ghost dance they painted their faces red. Red items like painted bones, stones and cloths, which were distributed by the medicine man, were regarded as lucky charms.

Red is also the lucky colour for the Papuans in New Guinea who are so interesting for us because they still live like in the Stone Age.

The Maori, the original inhabitants of New Zealand used to paint the houses of their chiefs and their war canoes red. For special occasions and celebrations the whole families of the chiefs were plunged into red colour.

In medieval Europe red became the political bone of contention: during the Peasant Wars there was a bitter fight about the right to wear a red "Schaube" (a widely known piece of clothing, a coat that was open at the front). Until then, this privilege had been reserved to rich people exclusively.

Henceforth the red colour was used more and more to signal political radicalism. The red Jacobin cap in the French Revolution (which was based on the head gear of the galley slaves) as well as the red flags, the red shirts sported by the Italian franctireurs led by Garibaldi or the red cloves in buttonholes these days the signal character of the colour has always been perceived correctly up to this day: as a sign for the active determination of the people who wear the colour and a provocation for the political antagonists. The most recent top-level example is the "red phone", which can decide about all our lives and death via the "hot wire" between Washington and Moscow.
We could easily add endless examples for the typical character of the colour red that runs through history like a "red thread" but this would go beyond the scope of this book. Therefore, let us leave it at this overview and let us direct our attention to another important field of experience.

The chromatics which are used in painting and design attribute the following characteristics to the colour red: power, vitality, dynamics. Red is obtrusive without restraint, it conveys the impression of warmth, benevolence and even allurement. The colour is rather allocated to the male than the female principle (according to C. G. Jung), a younger rather than an older person, the extrovert rather than the introvert, the southern rather than the northern hemisphere. Red attracts the eyes, no matter if you want or not. Therefore, red has a strong signal character which

plays an important role in traffic signs (prohibition signs are usually red) as well as in advertising.
Red suggests powerful health, energy, confidence and efficiency. It's a colour which whets one's appetite (also the sexual appetite) and is therefore used for the packaging of sweets as well as hot and spicy food. Tests with a so called "swift selection platform" (a curtain only rises for seconds and the test person has to pick the "most correct" package spontaneously) have proven over and over again that red (followed by orange) attracts the most attention in the shortest period of time.
Let us look at an example from press advertising: The only difference between three completely identical text adverts for detergents was the colour of the small packages depicted in the advert (red, blue and yellow). This small difference led to extremely different reactions. The advert with the red package was regarded as "informative, up to date, modern, reliable (!), offering something new, scientific, technical, interesting, vital, fresh, attractive, young and specific". The advert with the blue package was rated as "too boring and too shy", and the one with the yellow package as "too weak" (according to Favre and November).
At this point, however, it is important to emphasize the following basic criteria:
1. Only very rarely a colour stands all by itself. Usually, we have combinations of various colours which complement each other in harmony (colour harmony, concord of colours) or re-enforce each other in contrast (colour contrast).

For example, black increases the effect of red considerably, yellow makes red warmer, more dynamic and more communicative, green-blue makes a strong contrast to the colour which lets red look like inflamed fire.

2. No colour can be assigned to the stereotypes "good" or "bad". Rather, the whole spectrum of the possible impressions of a single colour ranges between two contrasting poles. Red, for example, can range from life-denying (aggression, killing signal, murderous frenzy) to completely life-affirming (vitality, love, health). This shows that we can only describe the general nature of the colour red (i.e. excitement) which becomes manifest in a variety of different characteristics.

3. Red is not the name of a specific colour but rather a general term (a term like "sports", for example) which allows for numerous shades, nuances and variations.

With increasing darkness red becomes deeper and more ostentatious. With increasing lightness the colour becomes the more spirited, merrier and the more imaginative.

Purple red, however, appears strict, traditional, rich, and mighty and exudes dignity. It's the colour of incarnation, the symbol of the paternal-divine, the "cold" red of the Cardinals – in contrast to the loud, hot and active blazing red. Purple red triggers the following associations – grand, mighty, dignified, king, judge, office, entitlement, ceremony, grandiose and valuable.

With a higher proportion of yellow and orange red becomes more provocative.
A proportion of blue up to the point where the colour changes to the enigmatic violet and lilac will change the impression completely (see chapter violet). In the same way as red changes to brownish, “excitement” passes into “calmness” and the “exciting blaze” is replaced by “comfortable warmth”. Warm Bordeaux, Burgundy or auburn have hardly any typical characteristics of red but instead many traits of the colour brown (see chapter brown). Pink is regarded by many painters as shy, sweetish, playfully romantic and soft. Pink lacks vitality, it’s rather coy and gentle, tender and cosy. Pink affects the inside rather than the outside; therefore the colour is preferred by introvert people and stimulates motherly care. The immediate associations are: tender, shy, maiden, sweet, sweetish, odorant, fine, quiet, mild, lingerie, spring blossoms, ballet, and cosmetics.
It’s hard to imagine a protest march with pink flags, a boxer with pink gloves or a torero using a pink cloth in a bull fight.
Packaging design and advertising are aware of the impression of pink and use it when care and tenderness are involved, for body care and baby products, soft detergents (for example fabric softener) and explicitly “non-aggressive” medication.

Above we determined that the physiological (i.e. body-related) effect of the colour red is excitement. All physiological processes are speeded up, the autonomic nervous system is directly affected. To understand this phenomenon, we should do a trip into the world of medicine.

The plexus of the human body is a complicated interdependent, balance seeking regulation system which is controlled by two main nerve systems, the vagus nerve and the sympathetic nervous system. While the nervus vagus has a calming effect, the nervus sympaticus has a stimulating function. Together they trigger all automatic body functions in a well balanced interaction such as breathing, digestion, pulse rate, blood pressure, perspiration etc.

In the event of danger and unusual strain the nervus sympaticus takes over control, causes hormones (for example adrenaline) to be released into the blood thus causing the body to go on alert. This process is usually called stress. When the dangerous situation is over, the vagus nerve ensures that the organism returns to a normal, stable level. Apparently, red affects the sympaticus directly and excites the body in a stress-like manner.

Studies have shown (Nienstedt) that physiological reactions to colours do not last for unlimited periods. After an initial surge of excitement the bodily functions gradually return to normal. Obviously, we get used to even extreme stimulus caused by colours.

When a colour can instigate such obvious body reactions (like stress) – how strong must then the psychological effect be? Professor Max Lüscher (the inventor of the self named colour test) et al makes the following assessment: Red means activity. "The individual who accepts the exciting sensation of red a sense of delight will regard red as powerful strength.

People who approve of red consider red to be stimulating, activating, conquering and expansive desiring. Red is appetite in all manifestations from hot love to greedy usurpation … red relates to the active part of power: the conquering." Thus red relates to unlimited self-esteem, the confidence in the own strength and the own ability to assert oneself.
However, people who reject red find it unsettling and agonizing. "The strength of the colour is perceived as threatening, red causes over stimulation and nausea, i.e. the exact opposite of the alluring appetite." (Lüscher).
The Lüscher colour test has been in use for about forty years – in such different fields as experimental psychology, medicine, packaging design and advertisement. Many different tests with very interesting results have been published since. Just to name a few in telegraphic style:
Women whose favourite colour was red, suddenly entirely rejected red when they became pregnant (H.Klar) and chose yellow, blue and green instead. They wanted for "stress relief" and hoped that their expectations would be fulfilled (H.Klar).
In situations where tension is high, for example before exams or tests, red clearly loses out in favour of its antipole blue. Other examples for this behaviour are European remigrants from the war zone Vietnam on board a ship (Klar) and prisoners of war who had spent years behind barbed wire in life threatening situations (Paul).
Smokers of so called "heavy "brands, however, have a striking preference for red. "Here the stimulus of

smoking seems to be used as defence against limpness" (Lüscher)

Coffee drinkers rate the same coffee as mild when it comes from a blue pot, too strong when it comes from a brown pot and as aromatic and strong when it comes from a red pot. (Favre/November).

Sensitive, slightly introvert people are rather deterred by the brutally explicit red. The optimists among them admit that they usually see things a bit more beautiful than they actually are; they look at the world through "rose coloured glasses"

We could list numerous more examples but the overview already illustrates the characteristics the colour red owns or addresses, as well as the colour's impact on the human psyche.

Let us sum it up:

Red is the most active and attractive signal colour, it catches the eye immediately and wants to be seen. In terms of psychology red correlates to the strong willed type, the quick-tempered choleric person, it's also a symbol for strong virility, conquest, power and claim to power.

Dark purple red, however, gives the impression of severity and dignity, grace and charm (Goethe).

Carmine represents strength and passionate power, vermilion stands for erupting force, while yellow-red even increases this effect to violent (Pawlik).

While bluish red hues appear to be stable, consistent and controlled, lilac and violet seem to be more sensual and seducible, soft pastel pink more tender and caring and brownish red more soothing.

In accordance with these characteristics the colours have an impact on people. People with similar disposition affirm these characteristics or reject them in a defence reaction. The funny thing about this is that the overwhelming majority of us behave according to these patterns notwithstanding the frequently reiterated myth of the "individual taste".

Once a friend of mine, who was in a bad mood, said that he did not think much of psychology in general and colour psychology in particular, because it was all much too exaggerated and the sheer mumbo jumbo – then he went to the cinema and watched "Death Wish (Translator's note: In Germany the title of the movie is "Ein Mann Sieht Rot" – a man sees red – which is a metaphor for someone being furious and losing control, completely). After seeing the movie, he felt much better, the main actor had "shot" his thoughts. This is also a case of red. Red – Many facets of a colour whose triumphant success in the history of mankind began with the three primordial experiences love, fire and blood.

The Colour Blue

Take your time, sit back, relax and allow yourself to let this chapter sink in calmly. Blue requires some receptiveness and a certain willingness to get involved in meditation.
Do you remember the time when your mind was at ease and you felt the "breath of nature" far away from the hustle and bustle of everyday life? You are lying on your back in the grass of a meadow some summer day and gaze into the blue sky. Only a few white fleecy clouds are floating in the weightless blue which is so infinite that your gaze is sinking into it like into the sea. The playful clouds make you dream and the blue of the sky seems to expand into infinity like in the song by Reinhard Mey: "Above the clouds freedom must be without limits"
We have a similar experience when we are on a holiday and sit on a rock or a dune on the seaside and gaze across the incomprehensible vastness of the water. We watch the horizon arching and we reckon that there are the coasts of foreign islands, continents and countries somewhere out there although we know that behind the arch there is water, more water and still more water.

In the old days, men must have felt like us – the early fishermen and sea men who felt the urge to go out there and explore the vastness of the sea – and all those who dreamed the big dream of mankind – the dream of being able to fly. The calm and endless blue awakens the yearning in us to follow it, just as Goethe describes it in his "Theory of Colours", "This colour has a strange, almost unspeakable effect upon the eye. Like we love to chase a pleasant thing that flees us, in the same way we like to look at blue because it does not put any pressure on us but rather drags us behind." When we think about it or rather when we are able to feel it, we understand some of the fascination which grips the sea men when they put out to sea or makes aviators soar into the air over and over again. Let us take away aircrafts and captive balloons, steam ships and sailing boats, all the inventions to feed the human desire to expand, and let us think back to a time when these resources did not yet exist. What will remain apart from the yearning? The endless sea, the infinite sky, in whose unreachable depth the gods and spirits had their home. This blue was inspirited by superior powers; maybe it was even the great soul of the world itself.

Remarkably, the gods of most religions with only a few exceptions always live in heaven or at least on high mountains (Olympus, Himalayas, Ararat, Fuji etc) above the clouds from where they could descend to the earth.

Thus heaven and earth are more than just places, they also represent body and soul. In my opinion soul or spirit are the deepest dimension of blue and all other definitions consequentially derive from this dimension.

As far as we know the prehistoric men's picture of the world and their experience of the world was a holistic one, they perceived the cosmos as a unity of the universe and all existing beings where each part of the unity was an all-one image and manifestation of the whole entity. Nothing was more important than something else but everything was relating to each other. Today we would call it "interconnected thinking" although in the old days it was probably rather a "mystical notion" than actual knowledge. However, people then knew about the cyclic processes of nature including the human nature and worshipped them. As early as millenniums ago in Indian scripts the world was described as a cyclic process and compared to the cycle of inhaling and exhaling (growing and shrinking of the world).

If we want to understand the primitive state of the human consciousness we have to take a closer look at the evolutionary development and the function of the human brain.

The brain evolved from the so called mammalian brain to the two halves of the neocortex, which are linked by the neuronal pathway and which are working in a fundamentally different way. Whereas the right hemisphere links to the limbic system (the older "emotional" brain) and deals with the holistic, the left hemisphere perceives, analyzes and identifies the details.

Under the microscope we see the following: the nerve tracts of the right hemisphere are quite long, their links are far apart from each other and they form a coarsely meshed structure pattern. The nerve tracts on the left half are short; they are close together and form a closely interwoven net.

"Although the right hemisphere has little control over the language ability, it does understand language and determines the emotional content of speech. If a certain area of our right hemisphere is damaged or speech becomes monotonous and colourless. The right hemisphere is more musical and more related to sexuality than the left hemisphere, it thinks in images sees the whole picture and perceives patterns. The right brain half seems to transmit pain more intensively than the left one." (Ferguson)
Marshall McLuhan says, "The right hemisphere "adjoins" information, the left one "adjusts" it."
"The left hemisphere deals with the past, it compares a current experience with previous ones and tries to classify it while the right hemisphere is sensitive for the new and unknown. The left hemisphere takes snap shots while the right hemisphere looks at the whole film. The right hemisphere draws visual conclusions, i.e. it can identify a shape even though it is outlined by very few lines, only. It combines the points and creates the pattern. Psychologists would say: the right hemisphere completes the coherent perception. It has a holistic effect (like a hologram) …
… In the classic conception of "heart and mind" – sensitivity and sense – we can think of the cycle right hemisphere and limbic system as the brain of our heart, of our emotions. When we say "my heart tells me" we relate to the deeply felt reaction which is initiated by the "other side of the brain"" (Ferguson).

Why do we ramble about the anatomy of the brain so much and what does it all have to do with the colour blue?

I claim that the primordial man's perception was more holistic than ours of today. He felt, thought and acted "right oriented", i.e. more emotional and more focussed on feelings.

I also claim that the left "analytical" hemisphere – much to the chagrin of all "emotional people" – has developed rapidly in the course of the mainstream biological evolution and has continued to form closer meshed networks. Today man is "left oriented", he subordinates salvation to the "logical" progress, a development that leads to increasing faith in modern technology and denaturalises man.

This one-sided orientation creates disharmony in the human existence, nurtures the "uneasiness in culture" and generates nostalgia, the "back to nature movement" and a multitude of religious or quasi religious reawakening doctrines, whose common origin is the yearning for the lost holistic life.

Blue is the colour which represents most clearly the visualized feeling of the desire for tranquillity, holistic life and harmony with the "all-unity". Blue is the colour of the feeling.

Most of the responses in psychological tests and countless popular expressions (which I value very high because they are sensitive and intelligent) indicate that all the previous statements are true.

But before we take a closer look at these interesting aspects let us go back to the old days:

The assumption that matriarchy ruled in many areas of this planet in older epochs is very controversial but nonetheless very likely. Numerous and impressive indications to sustain this assumption have been found yet. We also know that the colour blue played a vital role in those cultures. Even in oriental cultures, which are completely patriarchal today, we find blue at every turn as the colour of the sky, the positive spirits, and the protective powers of the universe. For example, virtually all window frames and door frames are painted blue in order to attract the good spirits to the house.

The tradition to wrap babies into blue cloth stems from the orient, too (in patriarchal cultures the tradition was limited to little boys because girls are not "worth" much. Only much later this tradition was adapted by the occident, where girls were wrapped into light pink cloth which corresponds to the social role of women.)

In Christianity the defeated and suppressed matriarchy still shines though: blue, the colour of the early matriarchal religions now graces the coat of the Holy Mother Mary. According to the role she was given, she now represents calmness and warmth, faithfulness and tradition.

As opposed to the sudden, loud and eruptive red of the fire, blue is a calm, yet even calming symbol of wholeness and for the ever recurring cycle of the existence. Water flows down into the valley, fills the oceans, rises up, mixes with the blue of the sky and rains down as a godsend blessing.

"The blue of the sky is reflected by the ocean to create the blue of infinity", says a Haiku (a Japanese epigram) quite rightly.

In all cultures blue has always been the colour of the spirit, the sky and the gods. The Christian God as the saviour of mankind wears (like Mary) the colour of the sky as the symbol of truth and eternity. In the Old Testament the colour blue is already considered as a special cultic colour. For example blue cloths covered the liturgical vessels in the tabernacle, blue was often the chosen colour for the priests' robes. Indigo represented the trinity of Father, Son and Holy Spirit and was as such mainly used for illustrations of the last judgement in romantic book painting. Purple blue symbolized the fathomless cosmos, the great secret and the salvation through Jesus Christ. The immortality of man was also often symbolized by the colour blue. In the Eastern Orthodox Church turquoise blue represents the ocean and the sky as well as the vitality given by God.

In the old Egypt dark blue was the colour of the water and as such the colour of the life-giving Nile gods, for example the great god Chnum who lived in the area of the cataracts watching over the vitally important bodies of water which brought the Nile mud which ensured soil fertility and provided food. Strikingly, the majority of amulets showing gods were crafted in green-blue faience. Blue jewellery was also very common for women as well as for men. The frequent use of blue glass (by adding cobalt) in those days came from the magical concept of the wondrous and healing powers ascribed to the colour blue. On special occasions and festivities the pharaoh wore a blue helmet to demonstrate his direct descent from the heavenly gods.

In China the colour blue symbolized the powers of heaven and immortality, too.

In India various gods are portrayed with blue heads or blue skin colour. An elephant painted in blue is regarded there as the symbol of utmost spiritualization and divine enlightenment. In Indian thinking blue also symbolizes the "heart" of the creational world principle. The state of matter at the beginning of the world is imagined as blue light (an idea which surprisingly brings to mind the discovery of the "orgon" by Wilhelm Reich – he also describes blue light which evolves from releasing the orgon, the force of life.)

The ritual use of blue was common in virtual all early high cultures but also in so called "primitive" tribal religions, for example in Central Africa and Native American tribes. A complete listing would fill books.

Now blue is a pigment that is found rarely in nature. The Egyptians used mainly the blue-green mineral malachite which can be easily mashed and grinded. Azurite (also called mountain blue or caeruleum) was also used but the colour was not fast but changed to greenish too easily. Much more beautiful and consistent was lapis lazuli (lazurite) which was found in the Middle East, In India and the Hindu Kush. The lazurite is a gemstone which was already very expensive in ancient times; it was kept in the treasure chambers of the Pharaohs. The Cretans (Minoan culture), the Greeks and the Romans were also fascinated by the shining lapis lazuli. The stones were grinded and used as a powdery pigment mass – this method was used until the late middle age which is shown on many well conserved frescoes and panels. Another popular name of the lazurite is "ultramarine". The name reveals its origin (ultra mare – from far over the sea). As late as 1834 a method was developed that allowed to replace the precious lazurite as basic substance and to manufacture much cheaper synthetic ultramarine which is used for painting today.

Another blue colour which was already known in the old day, is indigo, a substance which comes from the Indian plant "indogofera" and is very difficult to extract. During the British Colonial rule of India the indogoid dye replaced European plants (blueberry, elder, privet, sloes et al) which had been previously used but did not provide for such brilliant and intensive dyestuff. Indigo started a universal triumphant procession when the first jeans were dyed indigo blue (of course, the genuine jeans indigo was only used until it could be replaced by the now common synthetic colouring). Jeans blue is more than just a colour of clothes; it represents a visualised view of life: jeans blue connects people notwithstanding their gender role, age, racial or social barriers.

After this brief excursion to the history of dyestuff let us return to the sign language of the colour blue: if we examine the etymology of the word "religion" we find terms like "bond" and "universal unity" which are related to dedication, contemplativeness, faith and tra-

dition. In this sense, blue is a very "religious" colour. Blue stands for the everlasting search for a loving entity, the primal safety in the mother's lap.
While red is the glaring opposite representing the exciting fascination of the outside world with all the noisy details, blue turns to the inner tranquillity which is the only state of mind that enables us to perceive and comprehend the entirety of the existence.
Therefore it does not come as a surprise that blue became the symbolic colour of the Romanticism, a philosophy whose core was the concept of the unity of nature and its omnipresent magical effect.

In his novel "Heinrich von Ofterdingen" (1802) Novalis combined poetry, religion, and philosophy in the central image of the "blue flower" which became a symbol for the whole epoch as "the blue flower of Romanticism". He saw the blue flower in his dream and felt immediately that this was a "key experience":
"All sensations rose in his soul to a never known height … a heavenly feeling flooded his inner being, with heartfelt yearning countless thoughts and feeling called up new and amazing images and pictures, which flew into each other like visible beings around him …
Intoxicated with delight but aware of each impression, he slowly swam along the luminous stream which flowed out of the basin into the cavern. Some sweet slumber overpowered him and he dreamed about indescribable occurrences and he woke up from a new enlightenment. He was lying on a soft grass at the edge of a well which poured out into the

air. At a little distance, hazy blue cliffs rose with gleaming veins of gold shining through their sides. All around him was a softer mellower light than usual, and the sky above was dark blue and cloudless. What most attracted him was a lovely blue flower growing at the edge of the well. Its large glossy leaves touched him. The air was perfumed by the fragrance of flowers of every colour, but he cared for none of them but the blue flower, at which he gazed in tender adoration. As he stood to examine it more closely, it seemed to move and change, the glossy leaves bent down at the stalk and the blossom lent towards him, the blue petals slowly opened and he saw a lovely, tender face. Amazed at this sight, he was about to speak when he was aroused by his mother's voice, and he found himself in his own room, already painted by the golden light of the morning ..."

It is obvious that this blue flower is not a real flower (which was suggested ever again) but a symbol for something so all-embracing that language is not good enough to name it. The blue flower is not the goal but the road to gnosis and salvation, to love and the fulfilment of all dreams.

"You saw the wonder of the world" the father is told in his dream (in the novel). The blue flower is a revelation; it shows the way to the secret world of the heaven and the spirit.

This tenor pervades the Romanticism. Artists like Hölderlin and Novalis, the Grimm brothers, Hans Christian Andersen, Puschkin, Rousseau, Thomas

Mann, Victor Hugo, Edgar Allen Poe used the symbolic language of the blue flower as well as Wagner, Turner, the philosophers Schelling, Fichte, Schopenhauer and Nietzsche and the so called "Turnvater" Jahn.

In a famous poem Novalis described his view of the world as follows:

When numbers and digits
Are no longer the keys to all creatures
When those who sing and kiss
Know more than the most learned scholars
When the world returns to freedom
And goes back to the actual world
When light and darkness join once more
And create something entirely transparent,
And people see in poems and fairy tales
The eternal history of the world,
Then our entire twisted nature will turn
And run at the utterance of a single secret word

How is our modern culture criticised here and which intentions are behind this?

The world of materialism and its all too explicit manifestations is rejected as too presumptuous and superficial, the left brain half which is responsible for such a rational approach is dismissed. In lieu thereof the power of the mysteriously operating wholeness, which is performed by the holistic structure of the right brain half is upheld as motivating us in a truly deep and significant way as a counterbalance in our unemotional time. The more our life is affected by the factual constraints of modern times, the stronger is our nostalgic longing for a whole and intact world we can perceive with our souls.

Just like in the story of the "blue flower" the key to infinity is to be found in the individual.

The Nazarenes, the Pre-Raphaelites and soon after the artists of the close-to-nature Art Nouveau gave this longing an artistic expression. The paintings, sculptures and objects from this time are never just a formal end in itself or just aesthetic objects. They are rather considered as encoded signals in a symbolic language of an alphabet designed to interpret the world in a new way which is deeper and more profound that ever before.

In recent history the roots of the hippie movement and today's counterculture peace movement stretch back to these ideas. Their striving for harmony shows their longing for wholeness and a balance between rational technology and emotional consciousness.

In this context it is interesting to see that blue, which was considered as a very "female" colour for a long time and which is still favoured by many women over the "male" red, is more and more accepted by men. This change is another sign for the breaking up of strict gender stereotypes. After all, we know that all of us, each human being, has typical "male" as well as typical "female" elements in their soul, although the share and influence of these elements is very different. In this context the colour violet plays an important role as the colour that combines and mixes red and blue (see chapter violet).

Some comments about the colour blue:

"Silence is the inherent state of beauty like calmness is the state of the undisturbed sea." (Schelling)
"The inclination of blue to deepen is so strong that its inner appeal is stronger when its shade is deeper. The deeper the blue the more it calls us into the infinite, arousing a longing for purity and the transcendental. Blue is typically the colour of heaven. Very dark blue develops an element of tranquillity. When blue sinks into black it echoes a grief that is beyond human. Attaining an endless profound meaning in the deep seriousness of all things where there is no end … blue is concentric motion." (Kandinsky who founded the artist group "The Blue Rider" together with Paul Klee, August Macke, Franz Marc et al)
"While yellow is beaming towards the outside, blue is beaming towards the inside and contracting into itself." (Steiner)
"Lost in the distant blue I often look up to the ether and into the holy sea and I feel like a kindred spirit opens my arms, the agony of loneliness melts in the life of divinity. To be at one with the universe – this is the life of divinity, the heaven for men. To be at one with all living beings, to go back to the cosmos of nature in blissful obliviousness – this is the climax of our thoughts and pleasure; this is the holy mountain height, the place of eternal peace." (Hölderlin)
The following famous poem by Goethe is often quoted as exemplary for the sentiment prompted by blue:

"Über allen Gipfeln
Ist Ruh
In allen Wipfeln
Spürest Du
Kaum einen Hauch,
Die Vögelein schweigen im Walde
Warte nur, balde
Ruhest Du auch."

("Over all the treetops is rest,
A gentle breeze scarcely stirs their waving crest;
All the birds are silent each in his quiet nest
So my heart, waiting, soon will rest")

There are lots of popular terms and expressions containing "blue"
"Blau machen" (literally: make blue) means doing nothing, to have some rest and leisure. Most likely the term comes from old traditions of blue dyeing. The dye bath was prepared on Sundays and after 24 hours, that is to say on "blue Monday", it was taken out into the air for the oxidizing process which tinted the fluid blue. Therefore, Monday was a work free day for the dyers. The term "einbleuen" (literally: blue something into somebody), which means "impress upon, inculcate" comes from the same profession – in colloquial usage "verbleuen" for "beat into". Obsolete and no longer in use is the term "einbläuen" meaning idle away.
In a similar sense the often depicted "blue hour" is a term for the late afternoon leisure time which is dedicated to rest like a siesta and no work is done. The

“Fahrt ins Blaue” (literally: trip into the blue) has no goal and no specific route just like “ins Blaue hineinleben” (literally: live into the blue) means living with no goal and having no purpose. (Translator note: in English the expressions “out of the blue” and “vanish into the blue” have the same character of describing random and unknown origin and goal, respectively)

A similar expression is “in den blauen Dunst hineinreden” (literally: talk into the blue mist) which means talking about something freely associating without knowing much and having no concept. Someone who creates this “blue mist” for other people (anderen einen blauen Dunst vormachen), i.e. who makes up stories and fantasies to entertain people, maybe experience a “Blaues Wunder” (blue miracle), i.e. an unexpected response.

Generally, blue is often the colour of the miraculous, fairy tales, the enigmatic, dreams and meditation. Sigmund Freud and C. G. Jung describe in their books that the colour blue occurs in dreams very often. Something else, however, is the “blau sein” which mean being slightly drunk.

The custom of wearing blue clothes in our culture can be traced back to the early Middle Ages. The traditional blue indicated reliable stability, “fidelity” and the symbolic meaning was in fact understood. When a woman cheated on her husband, the neighbours said” she wears a blue coat” meaning that she at least kept up appearances.

In the world of flowers (remember the non-ambiguous meaning of a red rose) blue also symbolizes fidelity (for example forget-me-not) although the popular language knows some mischievously ambiguous terms about flowers which easily change their colour indicating the unreliability when it comes to love.

"Royal blue" was the colour kings liked to use for their heavenly shining mantles (next to the powerful red). The term "blue blood" for members of the aristocracy indicates their fidelity to the throne. Another interpretation says that the term comes the pale skin of the peers of "heavenly stock" with the blue veins shining through.

Representatives of cool and "reasonable" blue are the "blue cross" of the teetotallers and the portentous "blue letter" which is sent by the school to the parents if the child is not doing well in school (this comes from the blue envelopes used for official letters in Prussia).

In the English language "I am blue" means I am depressed in spirits, dejected and melancholic. The music style "Blues" is related to this state of mind.

In German the term "bluestocking" was originally (in the 17th century) a police bailiff or a police spy. Later the term was used disparagingly in many languages for women with scholarly or intellectual ability and interests who, untypical for the time, went to university and met in intellectual circles.

"Blue collar" (as opposed to white collar) is a term for non-office workers who wear specialised heavy duty clothes on the job. Originally, the blue jeans was a heavy duty "all purpose" piece of work clothing, too.

"Blauäugig" (literally blue-eyed, dewy-eyed) describes naïve, good-natured and slightly quixotic people whose most prominent characteristic is the innocence. This symbol seems to be universal. Many primitive races use it to signal their neighbours that they are peaceful. We know the white (biblical) dove on a blue ground as the symbol of peace. On machines blue indicates pieces which are not dangerous and on traffic signs blue means "free", i.e. not dangerous.

As to the physiological effect of the colour blue, we already explained the function of the autonomous nervous system in the previous chapter. Blue has an effect upon the nervus vagus which has a very calming influence on all body functions. The body is set to rest and recreation. To sum it up: The physiological effect of blue is calmness.

The psychological effect of blue is best described as contentment. Says Lüscher, "dark blue represents calmness free of any agitation … if you are in this balanced, tension-free and harmonic state of mind you feel integrated, connected and secure. Therefore blue represents bonds with the outside. In the state of connectedness you are extremely sensitive to differences. Therefore blue correlates to all kinds of sensitivity …" Of course bonds can cause considerable problems,"… they either manifest as clinging when blue is given emphatic preference or as a loss of bonds and depressive isolation if blue is rejected." (Lüscher)

This means: those who reject blue, flee calmness or a state of relaxation as if they cannot afford a rest because they are afraid to miss something important.

They rather rush into the activity of red like very many smokers of strong cigarettes, who expect stimulation and nicotine induced activation from smoking. Those who reject blue associate the colour with negative properties: too limp, too cold, and too boring. They avoid blue like a disease although they are the ones who need the effect of blue very badly rushing from one stress situation to the next. Lüscher et al found out that people who are close to a heart attack caused by stress have a distinct preference for the colour red. According to Eggert the words "I cannot afford a break right now" are a typical statement by heart attack candidates.

"Those who reject blue are missing the much needed affiliation that gives us content. As a result they suffer from restless and anxious agitation, are erratically driven to search for excitement to avoid the looming slackening of energy or even depression of this void and purposeless way of life." (Lüscher)

The Swiss colour psychologists Favre and November explain the effect of blue as follows:

"… A profound and feminine colour which creates a calm and relaxed atmosphere. The colour is preferred by adults and expresses a certain maturity which cherishes childhood memories nonetheless. Blue is connected to the inner spirituality. Blue does not want to waste away like red but wants to be perceived with love, not with boisterous spontaneity. The depth in blue displays dignified heavenly solemnity where rational contemplations are ignored. The darker the blue, the more it draws us into the infinite.

Lighter blue is less conspicuous. Its character incites dreaming. Its view gives us a feeling of freshness and sanitary cleanliness, mainly when combined with white.

Turquoise contains huge power and a notion of fire – but an inner, cold fire. Its freshness reminds us of a mountain lake in the summer."

Some spontaneous associations sparked by blue: passive, calm, far away, retreated, cold, wet, smooth, clean, scentless, quiet, sky, sea, yearning, distance, dream, melancholy, reflexion.

Among the blue colour shades turquoise is a special case. As the coldest existing colour turquoise is associated with clear, icy, smooth, watery, mountain water, mysterious light, electrical spark, impersonal, idiosyncratic, transparent and hygienic.

Thus turquoise stands for the psychological properties "cold" and "sterile" In order to understand its character we should think of those inapproachable, callous, clean upper class ladies who sometimes demonstrate the "untouchability" of their race by wearing a turquoise dress or costume. In New Wave and "Neue Deutsche Welle" (New German Wave) circles, where people act deliberately cool, unemotional and casual, the cool turquoise is quite popular.

To sum up it all up (according to Lüscher):

Blue represents symbolically smooth water, phlegmatic temperament, the feminine, the horizontal alignment, the festoon in a manuscript. The blue taste sensation is sweet, (that's why sugar packages are always printed blue). The sensual feeling is tenderness and the organ is the skin. Certain allergic

eczema can result from disturbed tenderness in love and family.
There are similarities between blue and green in some ways although green has a distinctive life of its own (see chapter green) and similarities between blue and violet. Violet still contains about 50% of the characteristics of blue whereas the counterpart red makes up the other 50%. The mixture of the two colours as a whole, however, has a completely new, unexpected quality (see chapter violet).
One last thought about the form – Itten (who relies on research about old civilizations) described why the circle and blue belong together:
"A circle is generated by a point moving in a plane around another fixed point at a fixed distance. As opposed to the abrupt, tense sensation of the movement caused by a square (red), a circle creates a feeling of relaxation and continuous motion. The circle is the symbol of the homogeneously moved spirit. In the old days the Chinese used circular elements to build their heavenly temples but built the palace of the mundane sovereign in square design. The astrological sign for the sun is a circle with a point in its centre. All shapes with curved and circular elements like ellipse, oval shape, wave, parabola and their derivatives belong to the circle. Blue is the colour that corresponds to the continuously moving circle."
"The full unity, harmony and tranquillity of the dark blue relates to the form of a dark area of a circle or a sphere." (Lüscher). It's no coincidence that both a water drop and the entire planet earth are most clearly symbolised by a blue point. Unfortunately, the latter

example is not quite true anymore. Astronauts already saw it with their own eyes: with the ongoing pollution of the environment and the atmosphere our "blue planet" turns slowly to grey. This should be a good enough reason for our right (blue) brain half to finally take action in the blue "age of Aquarius" in order to stop the insanity of self destruction for alleged factual necessity and treat nature with fairness again.

The Colour Yellow

Yellow is the lightest and brightest of all colours. What could be more obvious than comparing yellow to the shining sun? All children automatically choose yellow from the colour box when asked to paint the sun. Strictly speaking the sun is not even yellow but just a glaring light blinding the eyes when we try to look at him. Only at sunset the sun looks glowingly orange above the horizon.

No, the sun is not yellow but we have this colour in mind spontaneously when we speak about him. The reason for this is that we immediately associate warmth with the sunlight. On the other hand we sense pure white light as cold (and the sunlight is white as a matter of fact).
When the sun shines all things look bright and clear, the sun lets colours blaze and coats them with a warm yellowish gleam. Generally, warmth is sensed as very enjoyable unless it is too extreme. Goethe already used yellow glasses as a "psychological brightener" (mood lifter) when he looked at the landscape on grey winter days.

In his Theory of Colours Goethe says, "So, it is our experience that yellow makes a warm and cosy impression. The eye rejoices, the heart widens, the soul brightens up and immediate warmth seems to blow at us gently."

It is easy to imagine that the sun as the biggest celestial body has always been in the centre of human interest since the earliest civilizations. Most religions in this world have ascribed a fundamental role to the sun and worshipped him as a life-giving god (we still do this today enjoying the holy Sunday as the highest-ranking and most important day of the week, on which we rest and do not work. The same is true for the most important time of the year, the holidays, which seem to the equal sun and sun bathing for us.)

In many early high cultures (Egypt, Peru etc) as well as primitive races the sun (which was thought of as male) was worshipped as a godly being in sun cults. This powerful god gave warmth and light, let plants grow and ensured food but his rays (deadly weapons) could also burn and spread death and disease. The unfailing sunrise was in consistent harmony with the universal laws and a sudden eclipse of the sun filled people with horror and despair because they took it for the wrath of the sun god.

In Nordic cultures where people had a very strong affinity to the Southern sun because of the cold climate, sun cults were the centres of religion, which was manifested in Midsummer festivals, sun wheels and hundreds of thousands sun symbols carved in stone.

Known sun gods were RE (Egypt), Schamach and Nergal (Babylon), Helios (Greece), Sol (Rome), Amaterasu (Japan), and the sun gods of the Mayas and Incas. Apollo (late ancient Greece), Osiris (Egypt) and Mithras (Asia Minor) were also worshipped as sun gods althought they originally came from other cults. Many of these gods were sun and almighty sovereigns in one person and moved across the sky in a golden boat or in a golden cart. Their way led them from the East (Orient, place of birth) to the West (occident, place of sunset and place of death) and finally sank into the realm of the shades only to rise again in the East rejuvenated and reborn.

In this easily understandable cycle we can clearly see where the roots of the concept of the eternal life – birth/life /death/hereafter/rebirth – come from.
From the so called Amarna phase of the Egypt empire (around 1370 B.C.) we know the famous sun song of Echnaton (Amenophis IV who changed his name after the name for the sun – aton) which is one of the earliest poems of the world:

Thou appearest beautifully on the horizon of heaven,
Thou living Aton, the beginning of life!
When thou art risen on the eastern horizon,
Thou hast filled every land with thy beauty.
Thou art gracious, great, glistening, and high over every land;
Thy rays encompass the lands to the limit of all that thou hast made:

As thou art Re, thou reachest to the end of them;
(Thou) subduest them (for) thy beloved son.
Though thou art far away, thy rays are on earth;
Though thou art in their faces, no one knows thy going.

When thou settest in the western horizon,
The land is in darkness, in the manner of death.
They sleep in a room, with heads wrapped up,
Nor sees one eye the other.
All their goods which are under their heads might be stolen,
(But) they would not perceive (it).
Every lion is come forth from his den;
All creeping things, they sting.
Darkness is a shroud, and the earth is in stillness,
For he who made them rests in his horizon.

At daybreak, when thou arisest on the horizon,
When thou shinest as the Aton by day,
Thou drivest away the darkness and givest thy rays.
The Two Lands are in festivity every day,
Awake and standing upon (their) feet,
For thou hast raised them up.
Washing their bodies, taking (their) clothing,
Their arms are (raised) in praise at thy appearance.
All the world, they do their work.

All beasts are content with their pasturage;
Trees and plants are flourishing.
The birds which fly from their nests,
Their wings are (stretched out) in praise to thy ka.

All beasts spring upon (their) feet.
Whatever flies and alights,
They live when thou hast risen (for) them.
The ships are sailing north and south as well,
For every way is open at thy appearance.
The fish in the river dart before thy face;
Thy rays are in the midst of the great green sea.

Creator of seed in women,
Thou who makest fluid into man,
Who maintainest the son in the womb of his mother,
Who soothest him with that which stills his weeping,
Thou nurse (even) in the womb,
Who givest breath to sustain all that he has made!
When he descends from the womb to breathe
On the day when he is born,
Thou openest his mouth completely,
Thou suppliest his necessities.
When the chick in the egg speaks within the shell,
Thou givest him breath within it to maintain him.
When thou hast made him his fulfillment within the egg, to break it,
He comes forth from the egg to speak at his completed (time);
He walks upon his legs when he comes forth from it.

How manifold it is, what thou hast made!
They are hidden from the face (of man).
O sole god, like whom there is no other!
Thou didst create the world according to thy desire,
Whilst thou wert alone: All men, cattle, and wild beasts,

Whatever is on earth, going upon (its) feet,
And what is on high, flying with its wings.

The countries of Syria and Nubia, the land of Egypt,
Thou settest every man in his place,
Thou suppliest their necessities:
Everyone has his food, and his time of life is reckoned.
Their tongues are separate in speech,
And their natures as well;
Their skins are distinguished,
As thou distinguishest the foreign peoples.
Thou makest a Nile in the underworld,
Thou bringest forth as thou desirest
To maintain the people (of Egypt)
According as thou madest them for thyself,
The lord of all of them, wearying (himself) with them,
The lord of every land, rising for them,
The Aton of the day, great of majesty.

All distant foreign countries, thou makest their life (also),
For thou hast set a Nile in heaven,
That it may descend for them and make waves upon the mountains,
Like the great green sea,
To water their fields in their towns.
How effective they are, thy plans, O lord of eternity!
The Nile in heaven, it is for the foreign peoples
And for the beasts of every desert that go upon (their) feet;

(While the true) Nile comes from the underworld for Egypt.

Thy rays suckle every meadow.
When thou risest, they live, they grow for thee.
Thou makest the seasons in order to rear all that thou hast made,
The winter to cool them,
And the heat that they may taste thee.
Thou hast made the distant sky in order to rise therein,
In order to see all that thou dost make.
Whilst thou wert alone,
Rising in thy form as the living Aton,
Appearing, shining, withdrawing or approaching,
Thou madest millions of forms of thyself alone.
Cities, towns, fields, road, and river –
Every eye beholds thee over against them,
For thou art the Aton of the day over the earth …

Thou are in my heart,
And there is no other that knows thee
Save thy son Nefer-kheperu-Re Wa-en-Re,
For thou hast made him well-versed in thy plans and in thy strength.

The world came into being by thy hand,
According as thou hast made them.
When thou hast risen they live,
When thou settest they die.
Thou art lifetime thy own self,
For one lives (only) through thee.
Eyes are (fixed) on beauty until thou settest.

All work is laid aside when thou settest in the west.
(But) when (thou) risest (again),
[Everything is] made to flourish for the king, …
Since thou didst found the earth
And raise them up for thy son,
Who came forth from thy body: the King of Upper and Lower Egypt, …
Ak-en-Aton, … and the Chief Wife of the King … Nefert-iti, living
and youthful forever and ever.
(Source: Pritchard, James B., ed., The Ancient Near East – Volume 1: An Anthology of Texts and Pictures, Princeton, New Jersey: Princeton University Press, 1958, pp. 227-230.)

Here we want to point out the polar psychological antagonism of sun relatedness and moon relatedness. Sun, warmth and gold are inseparably connected in the history of mankind (that is why we discuss the colour gold in this chapter yellow). Moon, water, coolness and silver are a counterpoint to gold which is reflected in most religions (see chapter silver). The antagonism of these two extremes was probably one of the reasons why Echnaton failed to have his monotheistic view of an almighty role of the sun be widely accepted. Especially in a nation in which the moon signs (ram's horns, Amun) played a very important role and where people suffered far too much from the blazing sun and longed – understandably enough – for the refreshing coolness of the evening and night.

Today we understand this – we also know sun-oriented day persons ("sun-worshippers") as opposed to moon-oriented night persons ("moon struck").

Still there were religious attempts to establish the sun as a centre of worshipping even before Echnaton (and thereafter). This belief is described in an old Egypt fairy tale:
A magician predicted the Pharaoh Cheops the birth of a son whose father would be the sun god Rea and whose mother would be the wife of a priest. The gods themselves descended from heaven to assist the mother with the birth and – lo and behold – the child's body was pure gold and all people said: this is a true king … So it happened that a part of the sun was reborn as a golden child to rule over the people of Egypt. This parable showed that the Pharaoh was not just a mundane sovereign but he was of truly heavenly, godly descent.

What is the essential property of yellow?
"Yellow is emanation", says Rudolf Steiner. Painters say that yellow is expanding warmth, it is flashy, cheerful, gently teasing and has a drift to expand more than all other colours.
"Yellow leans so much towards the bright (white) that a very dark yellow cannot exist at all … if you watch a yellow circle you will notice that the yellow expands, it begins to move out of the centre and approaches the viewer almost visibly … Yellow disturbs people, excites them and reveals the character of violence which is expressed in the colour which eventually affects the temper in a bold intrusive way. This property of yellow which has a strong inclination to brighter hues can be taken to a force and height which is finally unbearable for the human eye

and soul. This can be compared to a sharp trumpet which is blown louder and louder or a shrieking high sound of a fanfare." (Kandinsky)

All these properties of yellow, but mainly the superficially shining and literally eye-catching effect, are even more conspicuous in the colour gold.

"Toward gold throng all, to gold cling all, yes, all! Alas, we poor!" says Goethe (Faust) describing very fittingly the mysterious charm of gold that has always fascinated people through all times and cannot be explained in a rational way. Of course, gold has always been precious because of its rarity. But other materials are even rarer without ever gaining the importance of gold. The only explanation for the fascination of gold is the fact that it shines like sunlight caught in the ground. Gold was considered as a part of the sun and therefore it owned the inherent divine power of the sun. One should remember that golden helmets, crowns and halos actually shine like small sun when they reflect light. The round shape of golden coins also reflects the symbol of the sun.

A small history of gold

In ancient times Egypt was the richest country in terms of gold. Many important findings of jewellery, amulets, and even Pharaohs' coffins made of pure gold come from Egypt. Towards the end of the Bronze Age gold-seeking started in other parts of Africa, in Asia Minor, and India. Gold was also found in settlement areas of the Teutons, Gauls, Slavs, and Helvetics.

The Romans, who had no gold of their own, only acquired larger amounts of gold when they conquered the Iberian Peninsula and incorporated it into the Roman Empire.

Through the bloody conquest of Mexico and Peru by the Spanish Conquistadores (Cortez, Pizarro et al) Spain got hold of unimaginable treasures. For the Incas and Aztecs gold was not a currency or means of payment it was always exclusively used for symbols of their gods and kings. "The sun is the eagle with the fiery arrows, the lord and god of the year", says an Aztec tradition.

They did not understand the "gold rush" which seized the white skinned conquistadores. After an unprecedented exploitation of whole sweeps of country the gold deposits of South and Central America slowly dried up. Only some reckless adventurers were still roving about the country in search for the legendary "Eldorado" where gold was rumoured to be so abundant that people could bathe in it. Of course, this legendary place was never found.

Instead, in the 19th century another gold rush began in the North American "wild west" attracting hundreds of thousand of treasure seekers, fortune hunters and shady characters. Similar gold mines were found in Alaska, Australia, South Africa and Siberia.

There have always been ambitious attempts to transmute common metal into gold. The first chronicles about such alchemistic experiments stem from Egypt. In the 16th and 17th centuries the alchemy spread all over Europe and was surrounded by a weird mixture of mystique, natural science, spiritualism, and philosophy. Many alchemists were searching for the "philosopher's stone", a mythical substance that was believed to be able to transmute all elements. Only few alchemists took the philosopher's stone for a hidden spiritual, truth that could lead to enlightenment, for most of them the alchemy was only an unsuccessful attempt to escape poverty.

A considerable list of more or less coincidental inventions that came about as side products from alchemistic laboratories proves that the alchemistic experiments were not all useless: Sodium sulphate and phosphor, the manufacturing of porcelain and ruby glass – to name but a few.

However, maybe they were headed in the right direction by intuition. In the mean time, modern atomic physics have in fact succeeded in creating synthetic gold – but the procedure is so expensive that synthetic gold does cost much more than the natural gold.

As irrational and as incomprehensible the overvaluation of gold may be – it does continue to this very day. To this day the gold reserve, which is stored in safe bunkers (treasure chambers), is the backbone and the yardstick for any currency.

Countless myths and legends revolve around gold. One of the most famous is the legend of the Golden Fleece from the Greek mythology. The "Golden Fleece" was the pelt of a winged golden ram which was given to Phrixos by Hermes, the messenger of the gods. Phrixos takes the fleece when he flees from his stepmother to the coast of the Black Sea where he is friendly received as a guest by the hospitable king of Colchis. As a token of gratitude he gives the

fleece to his host. From now on the fleece is guarded by a dragon.
Now Jason, who has to acquire the Golden Fleece in order to secure his rightful throne, comes to the king's court. Jason is also received as a guest and asks that the Golden Fleece is handed over to him as a gift. The king challenges his courage and presents some tasks to him to win the Golden Fleece: Jason has to plough a field with two fire breathing dragons and sow the teeth of a dragon into the field which would sprout into an army of warriors.
Medea, the priestess of Hecate helps Jason and outsmarts the dragon. Jason flees with the Golden Fleece. The betrayal is discovered and leads to a wild chase which ends in a bloody battle and the death of all involved parties.
The medieval poet Georg Agricola, who does not believe in gold as a symbol for eternity anymore, thinks that the legend of the Golden Fleece is a recount of early extraction of gold (using ram fleeces in auriferous rivers) and writes, "Gold is good for those who know how to use it but it brings harm to those who misuse it. The burdens in this world are not caused by the things we dig out of the ground; they are caused by the terrible ignorance of men and the blind and profane greed of their hearts." From the bible we know that mammon was worshipped by dancing around the golden calf. Many terms reflect the extraordinary appreciation of gold. – Golden section, golden mean, golden rule, golden wedding, gold medal etc. In the fine arts gold is used at its best for painting icons. The origin of this art is again in

ancient Egypt where so called "mummy portraits", i.e. symbolized images of the defunct relatives, were painted on golden ground. The later images of saints were done, accordingly, they did not show "real" persons but abstract symbolic faces which were copied many times and the shining gold made them look supernatural.

The Latin word for gold is aurum. Many words for gold are derived from this Latin word, most notably aureole (halo) and aura (in the mysticism the human aura is a visible energy field emanating from a person but mostly the term is used figuratively.)

Ever again gold has been perceived as the archetypical symbol for beaming happiness. This universal symbolic use is common up to this day.

Let us return to the actual topic of this chapter – the colour yellow.

We said that yellow has no depth, just a reflecting surface. It is the colour that reflects light which is falling on a surface more than any other colour. Yellow does not seem to stick but to glide over the surface and expand into all directions.

This description characterizes the psychological properties of the yellow effect most aptly. Says Lüscher: "Yellow represents the fundamental psychological need to develop. Yellow is preferred by people who are searching for changed and liberating circumstances where they can hopefully release the tension of over excitement so that they can develop in a happy way. They need the tension of expectation and the exciting stimulation of hope so that they won't languish from disappointment and depression. People who travel far because they have no home or are not happy at home usually prefer yellow."

And about gold:

"While yellow is already an expression of release and happiness, this significance of the colour is even more increased by the polished and brilliant surface of gold. Notwithstanding its monetary value gold represents the feeling of beaming happiness."

"Release" as a physiological and "change" as a psychological significance stand for the colour yellow.

Favre and November add, "Yellow is the most vibrant colour, it is also the most glary and cheerful one. Yellow is young, it is almost intrusively vivid and extrovert. This property is most apparent in the lighter hues. Other than in blue there is no concept of depth. Golden is active while yellow with a tinge of green leaves a slightly unpleasant feeling."

The latter addresses a property which is referred to as "yellow with envy" in a popular saying. The unpleasant effect is ascribed to a cold lemon yellow. Apart from "sour" other associations to this hue are "poisonous, artificial, dangerous, and pathological".

The associations to "pure" yellow are: sun, day, warmth, light, clear, moved, free, very lightweight, sound of a fanfare, strong, funny, glaring, curiosity, caution, nervousness.

To golden: vibrant, sunny, stimulating, warming, lightweight, sensation of light, cheerful, good mood, corn in the ear, platinum blonde, width, openness, message, youthful, social.

Reddish yellow enhances the impression of cheerfulness and contentment. Orange will be left out here because there is a special chapter about orange.

Brownish yellow, the colour of amber and honey, already shows distinct elements of brown (see chapter brown). Associations are: sensual, comfortable, viscous, relishing, cuddly, warm.

Some interesting effects of the colour yellow are known from the experimental psychology. For example, pregnant women who have been preparing for fearless child birth (according to Read) have a strong preference for yellow. Apparently, the wish to solve the tension of pregnancy happily through the approaching birth and to be able to develop is expressed by yellow. On the other hand it was observed (Busch) that chronic alcoholics reject yellow very strongly. Again the Janus head nature of all colours shows: hopeful people prefer yellow, disappointed and frightened people reject it very strictly.

Lüscher explains very clearly "Who rejects yellow as a result of disappointment is still suffering from a loss they did not yet get over. The exciting tension which pushes the individual to hope and expectation builds up and can become threatening. The colour test reveals the state of alert: when the desperate people clutch at any straw and try to push their luck beyond all hope they choose yellow one more time but now together with the coercive black" In fact, the colour combination must catch our attention because we know yellow and black as a clear and unmistaken warning sign: from wasps and hornets, packages of rat poison and as eye catching traffic signs, for example

the crash barriers in car parks. Yellow and black are not only an extreme light-dark contrast but also a clash of two colours with fundamentally different impressions which are worlds apart (see chapter black).
Another example for the warning function of yellow: all football fans know what it means when the referee yellow-cards a player. Yellow is a very explicit warning. The next step is red – the red card means that the player is sent off.
We know that children do not mind to paint the primary colours (i.e. red, blue and yellow) right next to each other naively no matter how much they "bite" each other. Adults have a much more complicated sense of colours. They often perceive yellow already as "screaming" and "intrusive". Therefore it is difficult to combine yellow with other colours: yellow and blue (according to Goethe the colour of fools), yellow and red (two colours whose property "activity" add up and create a "cheap" impression), and yellow and green (polar psychological antagonism between the discharging dynamic energy of yellow and the charged static energy of green).
Whenever yellow is used for painting or practical use (packaging and advertising) we find that the application of yellow requires extra care in quantity and quality because it is such a conspicuous colour.
As to gold – it is easier and less ambiguous to use gold. Gold always gives the impression of value, it upgrades the image of the content, it is powerful and concentrated. Mainly in combination with black and red gold enhances the exclusivity of each product, be

it cosmetics, cigarettes, sweets, or beverages. Golden packages are definitely more expensive than other brands.
Gold appeals to the general public who learned about the value of gold over generations whereas a in small avant-garde group gold is already valued less but the cool silver or platinum ("to know it's platinum") are met with approval. These people regard gold as trashy, tawdry and "cheap". Or does this behaviour already represent a new anti-cyclic leaning towards the moon and turning away from the sun?
Let us end this chapter with a thought-provoking anecdote about French painter Yves Klein who used gold very often in his paintings. He says, "the philosopher's stone does exist in each individual, it gives us the power to turn everything we touch into gold. The hard part, however, is to realize the gift."
He developed a unique gold-money-value theory: On an exhibition he sold eleven same-sized, equally structured pictures but the prices were very different. The only accepted currency was bars of pure gold. In return the customer received an "immaterial pictorial zone" Yves Klein wrote out a cheque with the message: "The owner can sell this purchased zone for the double price; the owner hereby loses his own sensibility." In agreement with the buyer the cheque was then burnt and half of the gold was thrown into the river while Klein kept the other half as the owner and intermediary of the sensibility." However, he still regarded the complete quantity off gold as "absolute intrinsic value" – half of which was with him and half of it was in the river (according to Hardy). On the

documenta 7 in Kassel Joseph Beuys caused a similar shocked reaction when he refounded a golden duplicate of the Czar's crown into an ordinary Easter bunny.

Is gold going down in our estimation? This is certainly not true for the vast majority. Prices moving up at the market prove that every day.

The Colour Green

"Green is life" these words are often written on boxes containing vegetables, plants and flowers in supermarkets. They are true in a deeper and more fundamental way than the writer of the advertising slogan could ever dream of. Because we all, our lives, our health, our well being are depending on the green of the plants. The air that we breathe is generated by the "green lungs" of the plants round us, foods are made from plants (even our meat comes from animals which eat grass and leaves), nature that surrounds us soothes our nerves – there would not be human life on this planet without green. Green is life, green grows, green comes back again and again – hopefully.

Yes, what would happen if the life-giving green around us failed to appear? When after an endless long winter the meadows and fields would not grow green? When a hot summer would char and burn everything without mercy? Isn't that unimaginable?

The Sahel is far away from us – the low-precipitation barred arid regions of the earth. But there has been famine everywhere on the planet at some point in time, even in our area droughts turned whole swathes of land into arid deserts and caused incredible hunger marches, real mass migration. People know that, they do remember. An ancient knowledge tells us that our survival is only ensured when fresh green sprouts from the earth again. It so happened that green became the symbol of hope for many peoples, the symbol of hope for life and survival.

Very different areas of this world, various races, cultures and religions share this sign of hope: the Christians whose saviour carried a fresh green palm frond when he entered Jerusalem. Islam whose prophet's green flag expresses just the same hope, a hope we can only understand when we know the vastness of the endless desert. The hope felt by someone dying of thirst when he sees the green stripe of an oasis on the horizon.

The fearless Vikings started a new life in the scanty and icy scenery of Greenland naming it Greenland because they were full of hope. We do not even have to go that far – it's an old custom (and has already been in pre-Christian, pagan times) to put up an evergreen Christmas tree in our homes in winter as a symbol of eternal life.

Lately green as a symbol for hope has gotten a new unexpected boost in view of the dying forests. A global political movement calls themselves GREENS, Greenpeace fights against the continuous ecological destruction and artists of distinction increasingly address the issue: on the documenta 7 Joseph Beuys started his "plant a tree" campaign "7000 oaks for Kassel", Ben Wargin has been planting gingko trees for years (gingko is a so called primeval tree, gingko forests covered whole continents).

The colour green is directly connected to the process of life and growth. If there were no chlorophyll, no organic substance could be built to feed the animals.

The assimilation in plants is a process to convert inorganic compounds into organic compounds producing the energy that ultimately all living things need. The process of the assimilation or "photosynthesis" with the important role of the plant pigment chlorophyll is still not completely explored. We only now that the green chlorophyll is a complex chemical compound which is similar to the red blood pigment haemoglobin.

The whole life seems to be composed of the primal polarity blood red and leaf green. Anthroposophists speak about the "red and green life juice of the world" and an "inner and outer breathing" (body and earth).

Primal humans were certainly not aware of this mysterious context. Nonetheless they realized that the colour green was closely connected to the vigour of the vegetation and gave rise to hope for a good harvest. Many rituals and cult symbols reflect this overall comprehension.

In old Palestine (Jerusalem) brides wore a green wedding dress expressing their hope for a happy life and fertility ("expecting"). It was not only a symbol: according to popular belief the colour of the dress has an immediate impact on the possibility of conception.

Generally, green played an important part in times of the matriarchy next to the other female colour blue. In the Middle East, which was thoroughly moon oriented (until today the Islamic calendar is divided into moons instead of sun years), green was the colour of the moon. The moon had an important influence on water (high and low tide) and the growth of the plants. The female period was identical with the lunar cycle.

Moon, water and growth were very closely connected and represented the love of live (biophilia) principle. In astrology green is assigned to the mermaids and Aquarius, to Venus, the planet of love, and to the sea-god Neptune.
In Greece the equivalents of the two gods were foam-arisen Aphrodite and sea-god Poseidon. Venus as the female principle was the allegory of beauty and harmony, love and bonding.
In Islam the prophet Mohammed incorporated the "principle of hope" in his green garment and led the followers to the holy war under the green banner. Up to this day in Islam green is a holy colour which is often chosen to decorate rooms. A recent example for the symbolic importance of the colour green is the "Green Book" by the Libyan Leader of the revolution Muhammad Qadhafi.
In Christianity green was considered as the colour of spring, the hope for rebirth and immortality. It was the colour of the paradise as well as God's mercy on earth, which includes the hope for rebirth. In the Old Testament green is assigned to the righteous and the chosen ones who represented the seed of the new faith and hence a new life filled with God's Holy Spirit. The use of the colour green in Christian painting must always be seen in this context, for example the garment of the evangelist John, Saint Barbara (sometimes the Holy Mother) and the Holy Communion.
The month of May (mainly May 1st) is strongly associated to the symbolic green. Most likely the custom of May celebrations stems from the Celtic culture.

The Celts believed that on May 1st the gods who brought salvation, knowledge and culture to the people landed on the coast of Ireland (the “green island” on the coast of Mayo). For unknown reasons May 1st has become an international holiday which is celebrated in many parts of the world. However, the meaning “Labour Day” for May 1st comes from the more recent history.
Like no other month May is a “green month”, it displays the awakening of spring and the excitement about the imminent summer. Often the first tender love sprouts in the “merry month of May” as was already described in this “green” medieval minnelied:

Grün ist allem meinen Sinn
Ist der lieb ein anefing.
Grün soltn allezeit haben wert,
ob dein Herz dir lieb begert.
Grün ist gar ein fröhlich klait
Wer es nach seinem wirden trait
Grün soll niemant tragen,
der in lieb will verzagen."

(Green is in all my senses; it is the beginning of love. Green should always be cherished when your heart wants to love. Green is a cheerful garment for those who wear it with joy. Green should not be worn by those who are afraid of loving)

In the same way the myrtle-wreath symbolizes the everlasting young and encompassing love. In medieval times the left side, the heart side was called the "green side" A well known German song still refers to this although we do not use this expression any longer: "Mädel ruck an meine grüne Seite" (girl, come to my green side). On the other hand we call someone who is jealous of us "green-eyed" In German language a common saying is "über den grünen Klee loben" (to praise someone above the green clover) which means to praise someone to the skies. Also the four leaved clover is a very common lucky symbol. Both indicate that clover is something special. Clover has not been used as green fodder for along time here – there was a time when it was rare and valuable. The four leaved clover is so rare that you are extremely lucky if you find one. According to an old legend Eve picked a four leaved clover and took it to keep it as a reminder of happier times when Adam and Eve were expelled from the Garden of Eden. Other expression containing green which are sometimes used in a degrading way like "greenhorn", "green man" or "still be green" relates to the grades of maturity in many fruits – green being an early immature state while the fruit matures from light green or yellow to orange, red and even brown or black. Hence these terms describe a certain immaturity of the person.

The tree is the universally best known green symbol on the planet. Everywhere in the world there are countless legends, fairy tales and myths about the trees telling about their annual dying (withering and decaying of the leaves and casting the leaves) and their rebirth (buds, fresh young green leaves). Evergreen trees are a worldwide allegory for eternal, indestructible vitality while a blasted tree symbolises death and damnation.

The shape of the tree is highly suitable to describe the connection between Hades (roots), the level of human existence (trunk), hope (branches growing towards the light) and the sky (crown of the tree). The mythological role that was fulfilled by the ash tree and the holy oaks of Donar, the god of thunder in Germanic mythology, was taken over by two other trees in the Christian mythology. In the bible two trees in the Garden of Eden are mentioned: the "Tree of Life" and the "Tree of the Knowledge of Good and Evil". Unfortunately, Adam and were expelled from paradise after eating the forbidden fruit. The had eaten the fruit of the Tree of the Knowledge of Good and Evil, Adam becomes aware of his "nakedness" and ashamedly hides from God. God then expels them from paradise and thus keeps Adam and Eve from partaking of the Tree of Life. As a result they remained mortal and all their descendants remained subject to the perpetual cycle of life death and rebirth through all eternity. In early Christian concepts of paradise the Tree of Life was a fig tree (according to the environment of the origins of the story). Later the tree was perceived as an apple tree and is now also a symbol for fertility.

A role of similar importance in art was played by the Pine and the occidental arbor vitae (Thuja occidentalis) which is still regarded as the "graveyard tree" up to this time and is often planed on the graves. In the

Mediterranean area this function is fulfilled by the Cypress.
Christ's crucifix was also associated with the arbor vitae. For example, some images from medieval times do not show a timber crucifix but a branch like from a natural tree.
The Christmas tree was already mentioned. A similar, maybe even more important impact can be ascribed to the Maypole. In Pagan times rituals of sacrifice were performed under the may pole which were supposed to fend off evil influences and to ensure the fertility of the land, the cattle and the people. Some think that the tall erected Maypole, which was decorated with coloured ribbons, is a phallic symbol and the dances around the Maypole are relics of pagan fertility rites. In some parts of Germany it is still a standard practice to decorate the Maypole according to its symbolic character with baby carriages, diapers and baby toys.
The palm is a tree which was highly esteemed in the ancient world; it was associated with advancement, victory, rebirth and immortality. In Babylon it was the tree of the gods. In Greece the palm was connected to the mythological Egypt light bird Phoenix who burnt himself and rose from the ashes newly born, therefore the palm was the "tree of light". The Olympic champions were handed a palm branch before they were given laurel wreaths. The evergreen laurel also was considered as a symbol for perpetual life. Later, mainly in the Roman Empire, laurel wreaths were made of gold. They were probably a precursor of crowns.

On the other hand a withered crown of thorns was put on the head of Jesus Christ as a sign of death. The crowning of the dead with wreaths goes back to Early Egypt and was common in Greece and Rome. Today we still lay down wreaths on the graves to honour the dead. The deeper meaning of this tradition is to confirm the belief in the indestructible circle of life through the plant sacrifice, the evergreen branches, and the closed circular form of the wreath.

Considering the vital importance of the tree for the human history it is easy to understand why people are shocked by the news that the forests are dying because of acid rain. After all, most of the affected trees are conifers such as spruces, firs and pines which have always been everlasting green and have always been the symbol of immortality.

"First the forest dies and then man dies" says a slogan which sounds so alarming because we all feel the truth in it.

On the whole green stands for the principle of biophilia which affirms life, promotes growth and development, no matter if humans, animals plants or ideas are concerned. The opposite is the principle of necrophilia which is devoted to death, despises and suppresses the living.

For Erich From, who coined the two widely spread terms, the wish for growth and development is the most fundamental form of the principle of biophilia, i.e. the wish to live and preserve life.

"All living substance has a tendency to integration and fusion. It is inclined to combine with different and opposite entities and to grow in compliance with a pattern." (Fromm)

This brings us to a crucial point of our review of the colour green. For the colour theorist green is just a mixture of the pigments of the primary colours blue and yellow. For the psychologist, however, green is a fundamental elementary colour. Did we say one – it is the elementary colour in the first place, i.e. the colour of the ego. To be more specific: the colour of the survival instinct, which strives to hold its ground and to prevail.

But green does not seem to be the same green for everybody. Let us look into this step by step with caution.

Surely, green does have a positive effect on people in terms of ease and recreation. Resting in itself green provides for the necessary counterbalance to our turbulent life, it invites us to rest and helps our unbalanced souls to find the much desired harmony. Therefore green as colour of the centre is a popular choice for all kind of therapies. Walks in a forest, the view of green parks and gentle green meadows help the patients to regain the inner balance which is necessary to recover. In the event of psychosomatic diseases (ands most diseases are psychosomatic) the sight of green has a healing effect on the psychic process and thus indirectly on the somatic process as well.

Goethe writes in his theory of colours: "If you take yellow and blue which we regard as the first and most basic colours and bring them together right when they appear on the first step of their impression, the colour we call green emerges. In this colour our eyes find real satisfaction. When the two original colours are equally balanced the mixture so that none of them is more perceivable than the other, the eye and the mind rest on the mixture like on a simple colour. You do no want to look any further and you cannot look any further."

Kandinsky commented in a similar way: "Absolute green is the purest colour that exists: it does not move anywhere and it does not have any connotation of joy, grief, passion. It does not ask for anything and does not call anywhere. It is an immobile, self satisfied element which is limited in all directions … Permanent lack of movement is a property which has a soothing effect upon weary people and souls but after a period of rest it can become boring very easily … passivity is the most prominent characteristic of the absolute green …" Kandinsky seems to confuse terms here. Passivity? Certainly he means static. Sure, green does not have any energy aiming at the outside, it is not "outwardly active", it does not radiate and it does not obtrude. It is just there. But look at the way of it being "just there": seemingly passive it entails the cumulative will to grow, seemingly calm and boring it joins all forces defining life – striving to self-fulfilment, the hope to do it undisturbed and the certainty to represent life itself and its invincibility. No, this green is concentrated, amassed potential tension just like a tiger which is seemingly passive and motionless when it's ready to pounce or just like solid bodies which are static at the outside but in the inside they are a highly concentrated texture of molecules.

I believe there is no better way to describe the ego: It's a relatively stable entity which loves a secure environment and few changes (which is therefore deeply conservative and affirming), which seems to slumber quiescently far away from the cursory superficial irritations of the environment (and wakes up only when the core substance is affected), in short it's elusive, extremely slow and phlegmatic, and still charged with so much tension that in case of emergency it will break through with archaic force.

"When I talk about green as a symbolic colour, I am explicitly and exclusively referring to pine green, which a rather dark and slightly blue. The prominent, strongly stimulating motion of yellow and the contrasting calming, receding motion of blue are neutralized and conserved in green. Therefore, green is static." (Lüscher)

According to Lüscher the properties of pine tree are hard, solid and persistent and relate to the feeling of inner stability, perseverance, consequence, self-assertion and self assurance.

When we mix green towards blue we notice that it appears to be colder, more solid and more resistant. This colour hue relates to the type of people who resist inner and outer temptations, who stick to their convictions and have a solid self respect according to the motto "Do right and fear no man". – "Firmness of conviction and ethic integrity are the true foundations of self respect, genuine appreciation and moral authority. The psychological significance of green is authority as prestige and dignity, as passive side of power, as property and dominated territory.

Whenever the inner stability of green is missing and if therefore there is a lack of integrity, dignity and authority, they will be pretended to all appearances, with the demeanour of dignity, with material or spiritual snobbery. Prestige becomes a mere pose. Those craving for recognition use the status symbols in order to pretend authority. They put themselves in the limelight, throw the spotlight on themselves, they mime stability, grandeur, dignity and prestige. Those who lack the genuine self respect, the inner stability of green, sacrifice a great part of their lives to their egotism, their craving of recognition and prestige" (Lüscher)

Studies have shown that adolescents in puberty have a strong preference for pure green but reject pastel green. The explanation for this phenomenon can be found (according to Frieling) in the relationship of the juvenile's identity to the environment, the adolescent is developing to an individual personality.

In the chapter "red" we already mentioned a study (H. Klar) about European Vietnam remigrants who rejected red conspicuously often. The first colour they named in colour tests was green. Most obvious in their choices was the repression of all feelings, mainly sexual and physical relations, which seems to be quite adequate to the uncertainty of their future. The ego-related tendencies of egotism and self-assertion were clearly predominant.

Summing up we can say that the psychological effect of green is perseverance, willpower and dormant power, but also calmness and harmony.

The reason why Goethe and Kandinsky took such a different view of green other than Lüscher, Frieling et al is that they referred to different hues of green – that is to say a sated, warm green whereas the latter used a rather cool and bluish green.
The characteristics of the various hues of green:
Yellow-green owns much of the activity of yellow and therefore it has stimulating, cheerful, almost intrusive, warm, natural, bright, easy-going, and harmless effects. It is the typical colour of the timid beginning, the growth, immaturity, the colour of the first leaves in spring to the unmistakable gaudy green of the month of May.
The yellow green appears sunnier and warmer when it has more yellow parts but it can switch completely very quickly and get a cold lemon sour expression. Then it looks rather poisonous, dangerous and even ill. In the middle ages a sallow bilious green was considered as the colour of illness, leprosy, decay, death and betrayal.
The transition from one characteristic to the other is smooth, fine tuning is important. A hue that can be a nice "May" colour for one individual can have a shocking and threatening effect on the next person.
Neutral green, provided that it's actually well balanced between the poles blue and yellow, is a quiescent and soothing colour. It's the colour of the dormant possibilities – i.e. it can be just as passive as blue or just as active as yellow and since it does not decide for one side the colour remains static and has no dynamics at all. It is exactly this colour we associate with vacation, forest, meadows, rich lawn and

rest – anything that has to do with Mother Nature on the whole.

Blue-green, however, has a cool, almost inapproachable effect; it is reluctant, reserved and stubborn. A light blue green is called turquoise. In the whole colour spectrum turquoise is by far the coldest colour and it is regarded as distant and sterile (the typical hospital colour in an operating room), in a figurative way it is also considered as unemotional and unfeeling.

However, it always depends on the places where turquoise is used. In sticky, hot and humid factory rooms walls with turquoise painting give a pleasant feel of freshness. Likewise we find that in the hot and sunny south doors and window shutters and even whole houses are painted turquoise. Turquoise is also often used for beverages, toothpaste and menthol cigarettes.

A dark blue-green looks more resistant, robust and tense. The colour is often associated with obstinacy, hard-headedness, stubbornness and pride.

Pine green, which is a very common and popular colour and has a few black parts added to blue and yellow, is a serious and self assured colour (the colour Lüscher uses as the typical green in his colour test). The colour gives an impression of solidity and deliberate action. pine green is associated with fir forests and forests in general, including the dark, slightly eerie and almost lurking calm forest. All of this is embodied in the concentric power of the pine green which incorporates the ego and its claim to self-fulfilment.

Olive green has the colour of the olives as the name already says which means that it has a lot of yellow and black parts in addition to the pure green but no additional blue parts. Due to this mixture olive has almost a brown character and in fact it has many properties of brown (see chapter brown). Since the colour merges well with a natural environment it is used much as camouflage for military clothing and equipment, hence the name "NATO olive" which is used in military discourse.

In the semantic (related to meaning) use of the colour in the social communication, where quick and non-ambiguous signals and indications are important which are immediately understood, we know green as the synonym for safety. Areas which are marked green are safe, green buttons indicate that everything is all right and the green traffic light tells us that it is safe to move on unconcerned.

Green pictograms show us that they are helpful signals we can trust in and follow without fear (escape route), green doors (for example emergency exits) shows us a safe way out of a dangerous situation. First Aid areas are also marked with green signs.

Green is a good colour for interior design which was already recognized by Goethe who said green has a pleasant effect and is therefore a very suitable colour for the wall paper of the room in which we spend most of our time. Rooms which are painted green are very suitable as living rooms or studies which are supposed to radiate tranquillity and to inspire intellectual activity.

Green carpets in very large rooms like open-plan offices etc provide for a very pleasant atmosphere. Light green, grass green and lime green hues in dinner rooms and restaurants have an appetizing appeal (as proven by studies).

However, blue parts in the green colour, mainly turquoise, let rooms appear too cool, too impersonal and even inhospitable and repulsive.

Green light gives skin a sick, gaunt and ghostlike impression.

Green can be nicely combined with many other colours. In virtually every home we find green indoor plants. People in our northern latitudes, mainly in overpopulated industrial areas, have a strong need for green. Because there is a lack of green plants in the cities which are all covered with concrete, they compensate by hosting smaller plants in their homes. The costs Germans spend for gardening and for the care of their lawns are climbing to new all-time highs each year which proves that the handling of natural green is not only one of the most popular leisure activities, the green has also a very intensive aesthetic charm. However, in my opinion all the gardening and growing of home plants is still done in a very selfish and half-hearted way considering the progressive destruction of our natural environment. A sound environment is the only guarantee for the continuity of life and our future.

Hopefully, the human race will become aware of this before the damage is irreversible, it's too late to turn around and the old Indian prophecy becomes true:

Only when the last tree has died
And the last river has been poisoned
And the last fish has been caught,
Will we realize that we cannot eat money.
(Prophecy by the Cree)

The Colour Orange

When you mix yellow with red, you already see on the palette that something exciting, yes something tantalizingly new is coming to existence – something that blazes like yellow and that leaps to the eye aggressively like red.
That is exactly how the psychological effect of orange can be described. The excitement is not so obviously purposeful as in red but it seems to rather have an effect into all directions simultaneously: excited, forthcoming and bursting of activity. Those who bear it find a character in orange which is open and generous, intimate, direct, demanding and effusive. Here acts come from the heart and are spoken about with no restrictions. Therefore, orange stands for communication, warmth and cordial sensuousness.
Orange is the thoroughly physical colour of the Caribbean, the Samba, and the cheerful, forthright encounters. Orange is not so hot as red, it rather reminds us of the cosy colour of the open fire in a fireplace. But it is warmer more sun-ripened, more saturated and more complete than yellow and therefore it is associated with thanksgiving.
Other spontaneous associations with orange are: blazing, hearty, ripe, sated, lively, stout, joyful, warm, close, dry, mellow, roasted, cosy, autumnal,

sociable, juvenile, and vain. We recognize quite a lot of these associations in the garments of the Bhagwan followers who prefer a reddish orange, though. Due to the character of the colour such conspicuous clothing causes immediate reactions – either spontaneously approving (warmth, cosiness, yes-men, enlightenment) or declining (aggressive uniform, pushing, drawling).
In press advertisement the meaning of the colour is much more undisputed. It stands almost exclusively for warmth and ripeness.

The Colour Violet

Let us recall the characteristic properties of red: this active, pushy, loud and virile colour represents the way to achieve a goal in the most direct manner. Stormy and passionate, without wasting time on subtlety, rather aggressive and demanding and if necessary using violence. Red is certainly not picky choosing the means, it is more impatient than wise, more crass than sensitive, it forges ahead its wishes and desire and only stops when it has seized what it wanted to have. But what exactly is the goal of all this explosive passion? Provided the passion is not an end in itself (some people are really addicted to permanent stress) – the goal is arguably satisfaction and ease, the happy moment of victory, the achievement of harmony.

Blue, the ancient colour of matriarchy, wants to achieve the same goal by other means: through wise adaptation and empathy, by non-violent resistance according to the motto: soft water bursts the rock, by patient devotion and willingness to make a compromise even if it takes a long time.

The state where two contrary ways meet achieving the goal is called transcendence, i.e. the crossing of borders and interpenetration of two polar forces. Or as the mystics call it: the "unio mystica", the penetration, melting and the removal of contradiction and opposites. The philosopher and theologian Cardinal Nikolaus Cusanus coined the phrase “coincidenta oppositorum” – the harmony of opposites.

Violet is the colour in which the extreme tensions of the basic colours red and blue, the heat of the fire and the coldness of the icy water mix in a way that the potential effect of two opposites neutralise each other so that they freeze in place in expectation. Therefore, violet is the most peculiar, fascinating and mysterious colour we know.
Violet is the colour of magic, witch craft and mystique. Borders are crossed here too, namely the border between material and spiritual world. The wizard, the shaman, the witch are border crossers between wilderness and civilization, between the unbeknown, eerie realm of the spirits, ghosts and demons and the normal and familiar every day life.
In the famous books by Carlos Castaneda the Yaqui Indian Don Juan calls the two realms “Nagual” and “Tonal” describing very vividly how difficult it is for the modern, one-sided rationally oriented man to perceive both possibilities and accept them as reality. Basically, Nagual and Tonal are the right and the left brain half of a larger dimension, in a figurative sense they can be regarded as the brain halves of the whole world dividing and polarizing it.
Don Juan, however, is sitting on the fence between wilderness and civilization just like witches (hags) in the Middle Ages (the “hagezussas” meaning those who sit on the “hag”, the border) and can look into both directions.

His state and the state of all wizards, magicians, medicine men and women is violet, that is to say border crossing, magically changed, and penetrated by the mystical unity of the opposites.
Lévy_Bruhl, who researched primitive tribe religions, speaks about a magical identification of human being and totem animal, a level of consciousness where human intellect and animal instinct are linked in a mysterious way.
Such states are still well known by people living in regions of this world which are still fairly untouched by the cultural civilisation. (e.g. South American jungle, Central Africa, and Inner Asia). Characteristically, the colour violet is extremely popular in these areas. For the medieval mystics, but also in many other cultures, the physical world (red) and the spiritual world and world of heaven (blue) merge into a fascinating mystery (violet) where other laws rule than the ones we are used to.
Very early violet became a colour of significance in the Christian faith where a person (for example a Cardinal) who wears violet clothing indicates that he is a mediator between the secular and the hereafter. There is a similar meaning of violet in Buddhism where violet garments are worn in addition to the yellow ones.
We find the colour violet in medieval church window glass, in the liturgy where it represents humility, penance and a modest attitude as well as in the violet amethyst, the bishop's stone. Gottfried Haupt called violet the "hidden secret"

The sexuality of red (male) and blue (female) is also neutralized in violet. Clerical dignitaries show with violet that they are beyond "normal" sexuality. Women often choose violet during pregnancy notwithstanding their usual colour preferences. In terms of psychology violet is therefore not a static bit a transient state.
Children choose their favourite colour in a similar way. Violet is very popular among children before puberty or at least before their sex role specific preference for red or blue begins. Studies with mentally challenged children show that they have an even much stronger liking for violet (about 85%). These children choose violet (according to H. Klar) to express their enhanced readiness to be fascinated ad seduced as well as their longing for magical-erotic identification. Considering their preference of red (strong excitability) it is obvious that mentally challenged children are fascinated by everything related to sexuality. They strive for excitation in any form and want to satisfy their sexual needs immediately even if they are not in any kind of emotional relationship (in fact, excessive masturbation is significantly more common among mentally challenged children than among "normal" children).
We can say that violet is generally worldwide very popular in cultures which are close to nature and in particular with the ordinary people while the affection for the colour fades considerably in more civilized and sophisticated cultures and among people with higher intellectual aspiration and higher income.

Violet is widely rejected in high technology countries in Europe and in the USA, mainly among intellectuals. It seems like people want to rationalize their emotions deliberately not allowing any disturbing border crossing into unknown areas of the existence.
Only the “border crossers” outside of the standard role behaviour choose violet deliberately, for example homosexuals (who call themselves “let violets” in France) and transvestites. Those who were contemptuously stigmatized with a “pink triangle” in Nazi Germany call themselves “lilac lusts” and similar names whereby the colours lilac and violet are proudly used as a sign of belonging to the group.
Just to put an end to a widespread error: violet and lilac are in fact two terms for the same colour. Violet is usually used to name the exact mixture of blue and red and a rather dark hue. The lighter violet is called lilac, the name comes from the Arab word “lila” for the plant lilac.
The women’s movement caused the biggest boom for the colour violet (lilac dungarees) making it a colour of fashion. Feminists cross borders, too, entering new territory, overcoming prejudice and leaving role stereotypes behind.
Not too long ago it was mischievously called “last attempt” when a lady who was approaching the menopause was wearing a violet handkerchief in order to demonstrate that she was not yet willing to be “thrown on the scrap heap”. On the contrary, the colour sent a subliminal but clear signal of erotic interest. Perhaps the tens of thousands lilac neckties worn by

the Christian members of the peace movement were also a “last attempt” to achieve the “return to life”.

However, we can take violet as an example to show how the course of history and fashion runs in waves. After a period of reconstruction and economical growth in Germany with an inherent overemphasizing of the material side now the “other” side, the emotional and sensual side finally claims its rights. Violet, which is the colour of transition, represents the mentality that promotes the change of the value system, namely the sensitivity.

“Those who reject violet are afraid of giving up their independence in favour of sensitive and erotic commitment and afraid of compromising their sensitive and egocentric ego. These people want to control their sensitive emotions rationally and before they want to critically gauge if honesty and trustworthiness are ensured in case of an erotic identification and a personal involvement in order to make sure that the engagement is worth the risk. In our culture there is not much room for violet, which stands for sensitive identification. Emotional companionship is replaced by the wish to gain prestige and superiority with all the forms of snobbism and rivalry. Enthusiastic commitment is replaced by the concept of practicability and safety. Aesthesia is replaced by the imitation of the fashionable taste” (Lüscher).

But just these alternatives are “hip” now. People are consciously looking for emotional community (even if it is only a flat sharing community), they want to be sensually stimulated, fascinated and carried away.

The fascinating characteristics of violet is does have this effect.

“Just like the escalation itself is unstoppable; you also wish to move along with this colour but not in an active proceeding manner but rather searching for a point where you could rest” (Goethe).

Are we actually surprised that violet is the typical colour of fantasy literature (Fantasy, Science Fiction, Para science), a favour colour already frequently used for the book design as a signal, are we surprised that fairy tales, mysticism and fantasy are all of a sudden “in” as genres in literature?

“Violet is the most mysterious, enigmatic of all colours. It is tantamount to meditative, mystical thinking that jealously keeps its secret. Violet is sad, melancholic and dignified. When it changes to lilac, it appears more magical than mystical and more ailing than reputable. Lilac is not so self assured as violet. It awakens memories of a forgotten childhood with its dreams and its realm of fantasy” (Favre/November).

Let us sum it up: violet as a colour indicates the following states: sensitivity, metamorphosis, willingness to get fascinated. With increasing darkness it becomes more rigid and strict, reflecting deep mysticism. As a lighter colour (i.e. lilac) it becomes more easily excitable, seducible and reflects mood swings.

Dark violet and light lilac are both cosmetic colours which are always immediately associated with certain scents because they remind us of lilac, lavender, violets and other fresh and delicate blossoms.

Violet is sensually body related, therefore it will be rejected by people who are brain oriented and rationally mature (and maybe emotionally poor at the same time). The colour should be used with caution for design and clothing because it often causes unwanted responses which can come form the most different and diametrically opposite positions.

Associations to violet are: gloomy, deep, shady, velvety, rotten sweet, narcotic, minor chord, magic, mystique, introvert, mystery, grief, mask, forbidden, intimate.

Associations to lilac are: feeble, delicate, sweetish, decadent, cosmetic, intimate, tender, soft, morbid, lonely, desperate.

The Colour Brown

As a matter of fact, the colour brown should not even exist – brown is not found in the rainbow, there is no brown light and the sky which can be shaded in virtually all colours, does not know only one colour: brown.

But still we are all familiar with the colour brown from aeons ago. The reason is that we literally stand on it and we have done from childhood. Brown is the colour of the ground, the earth, that is to say the solid and safe ground our feet stand upon.

The colour gives us so much safety that we have stopped thinking it could be gone some day or even get shaken up – which in fact can happen in earthquakes. To have our "feet standing on the ground" is so natural for us that we take it for granted unless we are "knocked off our stride" and need to "gain a foothold" again. Brown is therefore solid, stable and useful and for us it means the firm basis of safety we are so used to that we take it for reality as such. It is the actual earth but not its symbol (which is in fact a deep blue).

We can approach the psychological meaning of the colour in the same way as the painter does when he mixes colours: the exciting, hyperactive orange is "calmed" with darker colours. We get a low-key brown red in which the fights of red have been already fought, the weapons have been laid down and peace has been made in the dark misted brown. Brown is beyond the active part of life and represents life itself but in a passive way.

"Brown incorporates the vital, physical-sensual sentiment, the libido driven Id- control" (Lüscher)

We find that the physical tenseness of the sympathetic nervous system has subsided but not to the contrary (blue) but it has genuinely slackened. The only law here is the law of physical sensuality, the pleasure of savouring and enjoying. Although we find that brown is often regarded as a transient situation of temporary nature it would be completely wrong to call brown the colour of exhaustion. After all, most people regard it as positive and think the state of passive comfort is worthwhile.

It is no coincidence that this attitude towards life often is reflected in homes (a warm and protecting cave): lots of brown wood creates comfort and cosy hospitality (restaurants). Likewise in fashion brown colour (fabrics, leather, and furs) creates pleasant warmth in the cold season. The slogan "slip in and feel good" could be symptomatic for the brown property of clothes.

However, people who reject brown as unappealing, ignore the vital state of their bodies (according to Lüscher). "Other interests, desires or aspirations are so predominant that no proper care is taken of the needs of the body. The body is overstrained by either suppression of sensual and sexual satisfaction or by exaggerated sexual activities or by extreme ambition to improve performance. People who reject brown are hardly able to relax and enjoy themselves at leisure. Therefore, brown does not only represent the neural-physical state but it makes us realize if sensual comfort does play an appropriate role in our day and if the well being of the body is properly looked after."

Referring to the social aspect it means that "people who reject brown want to stand out from the libido driven mass instincts and want to be acknowledged as an individual personality. They need explicit recognition and want to be appreciated through personal attention."

This interesting depth psychological interpretation helps us to explain a phenomenon of recent German history which is still not understood by many: the so called Third Reich. In the Nazi dictatorship brown was the public national colour of the state. The origin of the brown uniforms comes from Germanic mythology which was overemphasized by the Nazis. The "brown shirts" deliberately wanted to remind of the "berserks", i.e. the bear hunters (an archaic brotherhood who used to wear bearskins). They considered themselves an elite like the berserks and being above the law. They even represented the law themselves, proclaimed the right of the stronger who is allowed to kill and even has to kill (based on their mystical faith in fate).

On the surface for the rest of the population they symbolized down-to-the-earth safety and reliability. But this was exactly what was missing at the time. Nothing was safe and reliable. Therefore, the masses flocked to the "browns" because they hoped to finally find some stability, a solid and reliable power. After 1933 they had to watch how the power became all-powerful and so dominant that the individual was stripped of their personality, castrated and overrun by the law and order machinery. In the end the "browns" closed the circle they had begun with their earthbound ideology ("blood and soil" doctrine, emphasis on rural settlement) – they did not stop until they had taken the cities, the people within their range of power and finally themselves back to "brown", that is to say into the ground.

After this excursion about the most disastrous dictatorship of a colour let us return to the typical characteristics of brown

Brown is usually regarded as a compact, "decent", civil colour which associates solid, slightly old fashioned and boring, motherly strict but reliable. Other spontaneous associations are: work, housewife, food, dung, roast, traditional home made food, hefty, baked, dry, crumbly, stuffy, chocolate, tobacco, coffee, virtuous, non-spiritual, rough but cosy.

From studies (H.Klar) we know that habitual opium smokers significantly prefer brown. Lüscher comments: "the dull and dim colour is often preferred by people who are in a conflict that looks hopeless to them. They do not want to think about it anymore, they avoid reason and rational serenity from fear they might be no longer able to bear the life they are leading. In an attempt to benumb reason they resort in primitive libido (brown)."

We encounter such kind of substitute satisfaction of regressive character, i.e. "back to well being" everywhere: the warm bath, where hours are spent relaxing or the luxury meal (also sweets as a reward for oneself), the bed as the centre of well being or the desire of townspeople to enjoy the "simple life of a country estate" (which means enjoy the pleasure of the country life without having to do the hard work for it).

While green emphasizes the ego, the soul, the will to live and the will of self assertion, brown focuses exclusively on the physical aspect of the ego. Brown is the sensual joy of the "simple life" and often more than that and even overdoing things.

People who prefer brown also display an overemphasis on physical sensitivity in terms of pain. Mainly hospitalized children show this unusual sensitivity. According to Cardinaux such children follow medical advice much rather than other children. They are oversensitive in regard with their own well being. Apparently, they lack all unconcern due to the absence of the mother who would control the procedures. They are afraid of missing out, not to be part of the game and not to get enough food

Flehinghaus, who researched the behaviour elementary school students, points out the pedagogical importance of the fact that underprivileged children with antisocial family background often choose brown as their favourite colour. He says that this preference shows that these children wish for social roots.

Considering the above it is almost self-evident that brown (in many shades) is a colour that is often and willingly used in Fashion, advertising and product design. Brown suggests full flavour, vigorous maturity, volume and sound provenance (tobacco, coffee, ice cream). Thus brown represents a “considerable benefit” which meets the demands of a physically oriented satisfaction.

The Colour Black

In the beginning there was nothing and everything was born from this, this is what the holy books of the Asians say. The bible says, “God said, ‘Let there be light’.

These sentences show that black, white and all the shades in between (grey) were considered as extremely important from the beginning of human history. More than any other colours (even more than red!) they were associated with principles which go far beyond the symbolism of “normal colours.

Black, white and grey are no “normal” colours, anyway. In contrast to the normal”, “colourful” colours (which are perceived by the cone cells in the human eye) the colour theorists call them “non colours” (because they are only perceived by the rod cells which handle low light vision and perceive only shades of dark and bright). The general public does not consider them as “real” colours but in fact they are the archetypical colours.

Even in the most primitive languages (which do not know more than two colour names according to Berlin and Kay) the terms black and white are found and therefore they seem to be older than the first “real” colour name red. This is because they represent the principles light and darkness, good and evil, which

are the big contrasts that always moved people in the history of mankind.
The assignment is always the same and it is always unequivocal: black is the colour of No, white is the colour of Yes. When we now first look at the colour black we will always automatically have its counterpart (i.e. white) in the back of our minds.
In the beginning there was chaos and void, the absence of light, the complete nothingness. Creation as the polar force brought order and worked against this state: the upcoming of light, enlightenment, the divine break of morning which fills everything with life and exists in the great circle until it sinks back into the darkness of nothingness and the end from which a new beginning can arise.
There is a never ending fight between light and darkness, good and bad, life and death. One depends on the other one, none manages without the other one, it would be hard to imagine the one without the other. Both of them together constitute existence as a whole as the Ying and Yang symbol shows in a very comprehensible and clear way. Almost all religions are based on this view of the world. They all know the dualism of conflicting forces forever battling with each other with man in the centre of the universe.
The simplest effects can be seen by everybody anytime: the alternation of day and night, light and shadow, good deeds and bad deeds.
Of course everything is relative. There is no absolute black just as there is no absolute white. – Although the rule says that the sum of all light is white and the

sum of all pigments is black this is a sheer impossibility according to the laws of physics. There are no bodies and there is no molecular surface structure that would absorb incident light so completely and convert it to heat that we could speak of "pure" black.

Joseph Beuys showed (in the "black exhibition" in Düsseldorf 1981) that we can approximate black only through experimental physical methods by letting people look into a black hole in a bended stovepipe. Any physicist will confirm that only in a dark bended room black can become "genuinely" black (whereas "genuine" is also in good approximation of the theoretical value, only).

But let us think this through to the end: even in the blackest black of the darkest depth we would not see absolute black because our eyes are not made for this. Even in lightless environment there is always a remaining 5 % light reflection left which prevents the vision of genuine black but offers a very, very dark grey instead. This phenomenon is also called "inherent grey" of the inner human eye (Frieling).

In order to obtain truly genuine black, we would have to assume "minus light", a manifestation that is called "black hole" in astrophysics. Black holes are zones in the universe whose huge gravity attracts matter, swallows it and changes it to antimatter.

We said that black is negating the light; it is the negativity per se. From early passages from the bible we learn that the Devil, also called Satan or Lucifer, was a fallen angel, a being who brought the light to mankind and went out like a comet. Henceforth the devil

"incarnate" was a dark evil force that was inherent in the matter as opposed to the pure spirit of God.
The devil incorporates the evil in the world, the libido of the body (sin), and the quest to acquire things and to change them. As the counterpart of God, who lives in heaven, the devil dwells in the dark bowels of the earth, the hell. The term "hell" comes probably from "Hel", the Germanic goddess of the underworld, who gathered the bodies of the deceased in her black realm and who also appears in German fairy tales as "Frau Holle". We are talking about the great mother, the life giving "mother earth" who gives birth from her womb and whose vagina is therefore worshipped (in cave, grottos and fount sanctuaries) and in whose womb all life also ends (for example the graveyard, or the abysm of hell, which devours anything alive).
The "devil's grandmother" who lives in hell in many fairy tales is a faint resemblance of the goddess Hel.
Hel is a goddess from matriarchal times. The devil, however, is a Christian patriarchal concept. He is described as an active seducer who incorporates evil and seduction in all their lucent fascination. Therefore it is not entirely coincidental that besides black the colour red is often assigned to the devil. The devil's symbols are always associated to the night, his attributes and his entourage are all dark: the black flies, the ravens and bats, the wolves, the black ghosts, demons and worshippers of the "Black Magic"
We cannot claim that Christianity invented the devil as the counterpart to God because his existence is described in many other religions. Greek mythology

knows the dark underworld called Hades, which is hostile to life, yes even annihilating life. Hades is the place where the souls dwell after death; they descend to Hades as phantoms or the shadows of their former selves. The Greek Hades represents the principle of the opposition to life, the eternal night, death and also winter letting die all life.

However, the potential of a new life which is present in Hades show that the Greeks already were familiar with the idea of rebirth, transmigration of souls, and eternal life. The polar contrast of creation and annihilation in the Greek mythology are also impersonated – by Zeus, the god of light, who actively shapes the future and Hades, the passive lord of the darkness, who guards the past.

Similar ideas were already known in the ancient Egypt and many other advanced civilizations all over the world but also in primitive tribe religions in central Africa or by Indian tribes.

The Egyptians called the bright life-giving and creative power "Ptah", while the counterpart was "Ka", representing the dark shadow of the soul which lives on in the underworld after death.

Osiris and the black Isis were also such counterparts who created a field of tension where all forms of life found meaning and order.

In the Indian mythology this dualism is represented by the shining god Shiva and his wife Kali, the "Black Kali", the great mother, the four armed transformer and the ruthless destroyer.

The gypsies whose legendary country of origin may be Egypt as well as India still worship next to the

Holy Mother Mary up to this very day the "black Sara" who is the patron saint of the earth as the main saint whom they worship each year in Les Saintes Maries de la Mer (Provence). Likewise, we know the "black Madonna" from Eastern churches and many parallels from other religions.

We said that black means negation, the incorporation of "no". This is reflected in many civilizations, adventurous customs and traditions. First of all there is the so called "black mass", a magical ceremony exercised by black magicians and followers of occultism who deny Christianity and deliberately invert Christian rituals to their opposites.

Followers of the "black magic" are mostly interested in the material side of life and are even capable of yielding an advantage over other people by using dubious methods.

The battle between black and white goes on through all the history of mankind, all their religious hopes, their fantasies, their poetic desires and the symbolic handling thereof.

A small thing like the chess game is already some sort of world stage where the tremendous universal struggle takes places en miniature: white attacks black and each time the battle is open-ended. We find the same basics in Merels and other games. Board games like this have been known since the Old Stone Age. For a long time they were taken for graffiti painted by resting shepherds. Which is exactly what they were and are – today just as twenty thousand years ago.

In fairy tales, legends and myths the principle good and evil always fight as substitutes of us and something that happens deep inside in our souls. Both sides have hosts of helpers like good and evil witches, magicians, elves, fairies, dwarves, light and dark spirits, demons and the strangest characters clash in the everlasting battle. For example the Nordic mythology was determined by an ongoing war between good and evil which will continue till the end of time when all forces including past gods, heroes, and souls will clash in one huge final battle. However, the outcome is already predetermined: an exhausting deadlock from which everything starts all over again. This battle of the last days is described the apocalypse by the apostle John, it is the main theme of Tolkien's "Lord Of The Ring" and all later fantasy novel as well as many science fiction novels. All the great pantomimes (Goethe's Faust was originally a puppet show) are variations of the one same theme. "Star Wars" is another variation of John, Dante, Goethe, Tolkien and Michael Ende.
Erich Fromm called the inherent basic forces "biophilia" (affirmation of life) and "necrophilia" (denial of life, from Greek "nekros" = death)
"Biophilia is the passionate love of life and all living … biophile persons rather build something new than preserving something old. They want to be more instead of having more. They have preserved the ability to wonder and rather experience something new than to find something old being confirmed. They prefer the adventure of life to any kind of security. They look at the whole and not on parts, at

structures and not just accumulations. They want to shape something and to interpose their authority through love, reason and good example – and not through violence, not by tearing things apart, and not by treating people like lifeless things in a bureaucratic manner" (Fromm)

Black is therefore the colour of necrophilia, the refusal of all positive, and a categorical no to all development.

"The will to destroy the existent is expressed by black. The black negation acts as opposition and also as authoritarian force against all other opinion and lifestyle. Black has been ever again the colour of the anarchic opposition or the forcing and compulsive claims to power. The compulsive claim to power is the common denominator of such apparently different areas like colour of death, colour of solemn seriousness, garment of a priest and sexy lingerie" (Lüscher).

All proverbs we know indicate this connection with black: "Schwarz sehen" (to see something black, i.e. to feel gloomy about the future) means that someone does not see any chance for something to end well. A "black soul" is someone whom we should rather avoid. "Schwarz vor den Augen" (black before our eyes) means we see only black colour when we are about to lose consciousness and we sink into nothingness. "Anschwärzen", i.e. blackening means denouncing, reporting and "whistle blowing". Black birds (mainly the black ravens) are widely regarded as a bad omen just as the black cat which crosses our path from the left side (heart side), Children are un-

fortunately still frightened with the "black man", a bogeyman who is a milder form of the devil.
Most of all black is equalled with illness, decay and death. All dangerous diseases in the middle ages were "black" – the black plague, the black smallpox, generally the "black death".
Of course there is a logical explanation for the origin of these names: clotted blood becomes black but there is more to this, namely the reminiscence of the final transition from all "colourful" hustle and bustle to the "black" state of death like it happens when mould, putrefaction and "black gangrene".
Finally, burning brings "black" results: soot, ashes and fumes are black just as coal ands in particular charcoal. Dead bodies that have been sealed airtight in a swamp over a long period of time turn black, similar to peat, coal and black soil. Black seems to be the final state of life.
There are numerous examples for the negative meaning of black: the Black Friday (the day of the worldwide stock market crash in the 1930s), black humour, the "black Peter" (worst card in a German children's card game), the black list, black labour, black day, black as night, black cap, black market, black trade, black sheep (being different), black hand (a political secret society in Serbia by early 20th century, they were the possibly responsible for the murder of Sarajevo and triggered World War 1), black money, black book (list of negative deeds).
The general public usually regards black as the colour of pessimism, misfortune and loss.

One of the "blackest chapters" of history is the Nazi time with the necrophile campaign of destruction by the SS units in black uniforms (additionally outfitted with skull and crossbones) who were the worst mass murderers in concentration camps and death camps.
The "black hussars" or "skull hussars" are even older. The "black troop" of the "black duke" (free corps of Duke Wilhelm of Braunschweig) disregarded the armistice with Napoleon and continued fighting. The "black army of the Reich" was an illegal troop in Germany after World War 1. The paramilitary troops of the Italian fascists under Mussolini also wore black shirts.

Now what is the surprising popularity of black these days all about? When we look at the punk rock and punk subculture the emphasis on necrophilia is evident. It's not only the black clothes representing the total denial of everything colourful and alive but they also wear accessories of violence ad destruction: cold metal rivets, metal thorns, skulls, razor blades, safety pins, brass knuckles, chains and barbed wire. Their isolation in society, the narcissism that comes as a result and the egotism revolving around their own selves is turned from the inside out and shows the state of the inside – dead, burnt out, without hope and cut off of all vitality. It's simply "no future".

"Black reflects the congestion, repelling and suppression of stimuli. People who choose black as favourite colour (in a colour test) revolt against their fate in defiant protest … the test show that only a maximum 1,4% of the tested adults choose the "non-colourful" colours black and white. They are mostly

chosen by people who are exposed to an unbearable psychological stress which cumulates in a crisis, for example a puberty crisis, by hospitalized children, and also by neurotics and psychotics." (Lüscher).
This cannot and must not mean that a black outfit, a black handbag or a leather jacket always suggest a neurosis or a psychosis. Black is of course also a fashionable colour which can represent three kinds of expression: elegance, grief and otherness. Black clothes indicate that the wearer wants to be different and deliberately dissociates him or herself from the rest of the world. The black limousine, the black suit and the black briefcase are meant to convey the impression of dignity and seriousness and to make a person stand out against the average colourful world. In the Mediterranean all women wear black when they reach a certain age, not because they are widows but because black shows maturity and matron dignity.

The furniture and material of public offices has always been black and strict (until recently when the "humanization of work" began). Black office equipment expressed the distinctiveness, the distance, and the outstanding. Black robes (judges) and working clothes (musicians, waiter) represent this aspect in a very noticeable way. The only exception is the chimney sweep whose black clothing (like the stoker, miner and carpenter in the old days) was only chosen for practical reasons, because black is the "dirt colour". We do not know how it happened that the chimney sweep (the black man) became a symbol of good luck. The positive saying "ins Schwarze treffen",

i.e. to hit the mark is another exception of the rule: hitting the “black” means to hit the bull’s eye of a target and therefore it means being successful.
The fact that grief and funeral ceremonies require black clothing or at least a black tie or a black crap comes from our vision of death. In the Western world death is the end, the fading of life into nothing, the final loss while in the Eastern world, where people believe in rebirth and the indestructibility of all being, white is the appropriate colour for funerals. In the Eastern cultures physical decay is not the end but the beginning of a new cycle, the soul – beyond guilt and atonement – enters the pure white light of the all oneness, from where it begins a new life in a new shape.
Another feature of black is that it makes all other colours stronger. Black “enhances”, it makes colours more brilliant when they are combined with black. This aspect is important when black is combined with other colours in fashion design.
Mainly the negative effect of black when it stands out from the colourful environment makes it striking and interesting to an extent that black is used for deliberate provocation and shock.
Examples for such a shocking and frightening effect are the black flags of the pirates and the peasants in the peasant wars, the black masks of the desperados, the black garment of Zorro, which became the identification of all subsequent lonely avengers and outlaws.

Unsurprisingly, black is often used in fashion, mainly as an expression of pubertal and late pubertal defiant reaction.

In general black is strongly rejected by adults, equally by men ad women. Only depressive people are inclined to wear black clothes. "The colour black's claim to absoluteness indicates something that is final and cannot be released or saved. Therefore black expresses certain constraints, ranging from a feeling of weariness to a serious case of obsessive neurosis. Black always indicates some kind of internal conflict, no matter in which area this conflict has to be dealt with … The rejection of black is also the attempt not to get frightened by something inscrutable but at the same time there is the fear of destructive events, abysses and strokes of fate" (Frieling)

Black seems to be linked to a certain primal fear which is the origin of the neurosis. Therefore it is alarming when children choose black as their favourite colour because healthy and vital children abhor this colour. This is hardly surprising because (according to Frieling) black turns away the vital and maybe even the primitive. Black is intellectual. It is the colour of theories and philosophical speculations right up to rigid theoretical framework which is hostile towards life. A child cannot do anything with it. Black is a hole, it is something inconceivable, a symbol of an attitude towards life that does not want to awaken but to fade away. To quote Frieling again: "It is safe to say that the colour black is always present in situations when a vital force is being replaced by a theoretical, constraining, formalising, and reducing force. No other colour indicates so distinctly what we usually call a neurosis."

For Lüscher the physiological effect is "congestion", the psychological effect "constraint". Therefore he is hardly surprised by the fact that black is rejected as the most unappealing colour (which has been proven by statistics), because people who do not like black, also do not want to renounce. Renouncement means "austerity and frightening deficits". Who wants to take that voluntarily?

Favre and Novembre take a similar view of the colour: "Black is dark and compact; it is a symbol of despair and death. It is void without options, an everlasting silence without future, even without any hope for a future".

The only "biophile" aspect of the colour black is the area of eroticism. In ancient Egypt and India black-rimmed eyes rated as eroticising because they had this deeper and mysterious look. Women have darkened there eyelashes over the centuries up to this day. In the time of Rococo black beauty spots on the cheeks became popular.

Somehow black seems to be fascinating. Black hair is considered as racy, black eyes as passionate and fiery and dark skin -mainly black skin – has a stimulating effect on white people (black is beautiful). Black lingerie is called "teasing lingerie", maybe because of the contrast between the black lingerie and the light skin which makes it look more vital and exciting.

However, the border to necrophilia is crossed very easily in the field of eroticism, too. One step further and we have the black leather clothes and the black metal tools of the sadomasochism. A perverted form of eroticism where black can only be called "death of love" (J. Fey). But maybe they are just tired of the surfeit of the colourful life which has reached a point of no return and makes them yearn to finally plunge into the abysmal.

Black – it's the colour of the absolute beginning and the absolute end. What lies in between is called life.

The Colour White

After the previous chapter it would be easy to reverse all described states of black to the exact opposite – that is to say white – but that would be too easy and would not do justice to the character of this colour. Because white is much more than just the sum of all light (as the physicists say), it is more than the "immaculate" purity and innocence (as the moralists say) and more than "tabula rasa", a "clean sweep" (the popular opinion). White is the beginning of all possibilities and at the same time it is the escape from the consequences thereof.

What does this seeming contradiction mean? Let me explain the statement by using some examples.

We had quoted the bible: and God said, Let there be light. The arising light illuminated the darkness of the nothingness and everything became visible. When we visualise this process, we realise that white is in fact the contrary of black, of nothingness, of No and of chaos that waits for ordering constitution, namely the light of illumination, the colour of the absolute Yes.

But it is also evident that this Yes can only be an aspired, transient ideal state and not a permanent one. Between primal matter and light lies the reality of existence which is even inherent in the character of the light and the existence is colourful. We do know that the sum of all light is white but we see the aberration of light in the prism and we realize the colourfulness of the world. Maybe we do accept that the oneness of all existence in its entirety results in white but we do not want it because we are fascinated and captured by the exciting colourfulness of the world.

Therefore, white is in fact not a "real" colour for us but rather a state which is open to interpretation. How we interpret white depends on our attitude towards life.

The decision about our relationship to life is not made in the neocortex, that is to say in the newer parts of the human brain, but much deeper in the old limbic system (see the descriptions in the chapter "blue")

"The choice between non-colourful colours shows the affective and psychomotor initial situation, the vegetative tone, and the psycho energetic level of the subject, whereas the relation to the object is missing or vague." (Lüscher)

This means that the fundamental decision, i.e. the black or white verdict (including all grey shades in between the two colours) is made in the deep layers of the human brain and influences and taints all further observations made by the neocortex. Furthermore, it means that archetypical symbol connections are already secured here. In the limbic system the fundamental decision in favour of Yes or No, fleeing or resisting is made, a decision which equals the primal colours white or black.

Black stands for resistance, stiffness, ultimate rigidity, i.e. negation of life which is mobile and changeable by nature. The essence of white is the exact opposite: dissolution and flight. An example to make this understood: A white flag is set up on a house in the middle of a battle – a symbol that is immediately understood everywhere in the world as the sign of capitulation. We give up, flee from the torpid, standoff situation, and say yes to anything that may happen but in such a passive way that it can be seen as a way of self liquidation.

This extreme situation is an exception and decisions of such far reaching consequences are very rare in the normal daily routine. In everyday life both black and white are used as fashion colours, for example in clothing and furniture design. A British study on colour preferences of car buyers recently found that black is favoured by people of "staid mentality", i.e. older people, mainly men who regard a car as a prestige item and want to stand out from the common colourfulness. In the study white was assigned to even-tempered drivers and it was chosen significantly more frequent by women.

Colour tests which are carried out under scientific conditions show that only a very small percentage of the adult test persons choose black or white as a favourite colour. This discrepancy of favourite colour and the actual colour choice can be easily explained: The buyers assign social attributes to objects (in this case the car) and value these attributes higher than their own emotions which are possibly obscured in the process.

The results of the black and white surveys become even more evident when people choose the indirect combination of black and white (in the colour test only a maximum of 1, 4% of the adults). According to Lüscher these people are often subject to exposed to an almost unbearable psychological stress which cumulates in a crisis. Neurotics and psychotics instinctively choose the combination black and white, also children in a puberty crisis as well as children in a hospital or children's home.

Before we look deeper into such alarming symptoms and situations, let us take a closer look at the historical and mythological meaning of the colour white.

"All colours come from the white which is their home and origin by and step out of the white by division. The farther they move away from the white the more colourful they become – the closer they move to black, which is the death of colours, the dimmer and darker they become." (Frieling)

White is the home of the light which gives birth to everything visible. This idea can be found in most religions. The dark female primal goddess mother earth is always opposed by a bright, male, creational light god.

In the I Ging, the "book of transformations", a millenniums old Chinese book of wisdom the two forces are called "Kien" – the creational, the sky and "Kun", the conceiving, the earth. This correlating and complementary pair of opposites also symbolises the polarity of mind and nature, heaven and earth, time and space. The graphic symbol for their interaction is the Ying and Yang symbol.

Let us linger in this world for a while because we will understand the inversion of the colour symbolism like for example the funeral colours.
In a cyclic religion which holds belief in the eternal cycle of life and rebirth black is only the colour of the end, but the end is not real and only exists in the limited perception of the human being.
White, however, expresses in Asian belief the dissolution of the body and is therefore the "right" colour of the physical death because the soul enters the Nirvana where it finds a new beginning in a new incarnation.
Christianity contains essential elements of this religion, too and if we actually would believe in resurrection and the eternal life, we would not be numb with grief when faced with black and "final" death and only think about the decline of the body. We would have to think about the continuity of the soul like the Asians. The deliverance of the soul from the body would require white, the colour of release and liberation.
As a side note – in the past white was in fact used as a colour of mourning in our culture. It was Louis XII, King of France who introduced black as the general colour of mourning.
In most known religions and myths we hear about light gods, other light givers and "white" messengers of heaven who bring "enlightenment" to the humans. Angels are depicted as almost transparent beings dressed in white and of course also all humans who have liberated themselves from the burden of the material world thanks to an expanded consciousness

and who have come close to the pure spirit of God. The agents of the good, the biophile principle and heavenly justice on earth are called luminous entities, "white" magicians and "wise" men. The similarity of the words "weiß" (white) and "weise" (wise) indicates a connection between white and wise. In so far "wisdom" seems to be the presence of "enlightenment". In the Germanic-Celtic myths where the numbers eleven and twelve were highly esteemed, the words elf (eleven), elb, alf and alb were all equated to white. Hence white was assigned to elves as well as dwarves (Alban, Alberich).
Roman languages also know the root word alb which means "white". It is in words like albino, Albania, albatross, Albigensian et al. In Ancient Rome an album (Latin "the white") was a white wooden board for public announcements before it became a scrap book.

In the last chapter we already spoke about the Devil, i.e. Lucifer in the Old Testament. As God's antagonist and the incarnation of the dark and the evil he is a necessary part of the wholeness. Goethe describes Mephisto in his drama "Faust" as follows:

"Part of that Power which would
The Evil ever do, and ever does the Good …
I am the Spirit that denies!
And rightly too; for all that doth begin
Should rightly to destruction run;
'Twere better then that nothing were begun.
Thus everything that you call Sin,

Destruction – in a word, as Evil represent –
That is my own, real element …
But I'm part of the Part which at the first was all,
Part of the Darkness that gave birth to Light …"

In Christian mythology Lucifer was the most beautiful angel God had created: Lucifer the Light Giver. However, he turned away from God and was banished to earth (as the tempter) and to hell (as the destroyer). He is the incarnation of the flesh that resists spiritualization and his followers who fall victim to the temptation turn to the "black" side and worship the eternal night. In contrast to the black side the "white" way is the path to cognition.

"White astrology has to be considered as beneficial, life-affirming, not patronising but stimulating" (Xylander)

The colours white and black are very frequently found in priests' vestments and cassocks symbolizing the renunciation of the colourful hustle and bustle and the abandonment of all physical boundaries. In the catholic liturgy white is the colour of the saints, the sacrament and the ceremonial consecration. Since the papacy of Pius V white is also the colour of God the Father and Jesus Christ who is called the "Light of the World".

The rituals of Olympic ceremonies still reflect the old classical thinking. Male and female athletes dressed in white (in the old days in fact priestesses) carry the Olympic torch through the "dark" world into the stadium and spark off the light of reconciliation and solution of all conflicts, even armed conflicts. The

Greeks envisioned death – the contrast to life – as the younger brother of sleep or as a genius with a lowered torch.

Another example for the expressiveness and inherent power of our colour symbol language is the wedding. The groom wears black and shows that he has made a firm and definite decision ("until death parts you"). On the other hand the bride indicates with her white wedding dress that she gives up her previous life innocently and pure at heart and resigns to her future role with no resistance.

In this context another aspect and meaning of the colour white is emphasized: innocence, chastity and flawlessness. The "immaculate conception" of the Holy Virgin Mary falls into this category as well as the so called "clean slate" of politicians (in German it's called "Weisse Weste" i.e. white vest) who use the metaphor to affirm their "clean record" using their power.

Cleanliness celebrates true triumphs in the public awareness of the high technology industrial nations. The slogan "whitest white of my life" to advertise a washing agent represents the attitude of people who are downright obsessed with a cleaning mania which looks very strange to the population of the Third World – apart from the fact that these people have more important problems than to care about dazzling white laundry.

Psychologists and therapists have often proved the interrelationship of obsessive washing and exaggerated hygiene on the one hand and emotional sterility and mental disorder on the other hand.

Consumer products advertisement responds to the obvious bias for hygiene and perfect cleanliness which can be found in big parts of the population and uses it for nifty marketing. Bright and clear blue next to the brilliant white enhances the character of the refreshing and antiseptic effect.
White as a pure and untouched state is also a universal symbol for the truth and nothing but the (absolute) truth. In German language the word for prophecy ("Weissagung") has a common origin as the word "weiss" for "white".

Favre and Novembre list more aspects of white, "white suggests purity, the unreachable, the inapproachable and the inexplicability. Due to the lack of a specific character white creates at the impression of emptiness and infinity. It affects our souls like absolute silence but a silence full of vivid possibilities."
"Silence full of vivid possibilities" – the expression reminds us of the white flag of truce which silences the arms in a cease-fire and opens up the chance of a vivid beginning. The physiological effect "dissolution" of the colour white induces an analogous psychological effect, namely the chance of freedom whereas freedom must be understood as being "free from something" as well as being "free to do something".
Freedom is lack of commitment. Lüscher comments, "People who choose white from the board of colourless colours need to free themselves from adverse circumstances." He considers white as the border region of beginning and affirmation.

This border region can be just as pleasant as sinister as we already pointed out. Very often white is regarded as cold and dismissive because of its total lack of emotional liveliness. It's a common saying to call an untouched blanket of snow a burial shroud. However, we know that it is the burial shroud which protects and preserves the ground beneath and provides the conditions required to allow new life to begin when temperatures rise.

A white untouched sheet of paper or canvas is an enormous challenge for the artist, because everything is still possible at the beginning of the work. One wrong dot or line can cast a doubt on the whole piece.

"White noise", the artificially created state of absolute silence in midst of other noises can have a shocking as well as a calming effect because of its sudden occurrence and its difference. The effect can be relaxing as well as stimulating.

The context of white is of course, important, too. In a hospital white walls look sterile and not very cosy while the white washed walls in Mediterranean houses look lively and friendly.

Last but not least, a word about the hardest possible contrast – the combination of black and white. The concurrence of the two colours and their contrasting brightness respectively creates a tension that captivates us because the constraining character of black is paired with the freedom of white. We live with this tension all the time, we are used to it. The page you are reading right now proves it, you see it "black on white" – the most frequent type of written

communication which may not provide for the best readability (see table “readability of chromatic fonts” in chapter “further studies on colours”) but it is the “normal” uniform appearance which is learnt everywhere in the world and therefore it conveys the impression of authenticity.
To quote Goethe: “For what one has in black and white, one can carry home in comfort.”

The Colour Grey

Most animals are limited in their perception of colour, they are partially or even completely colour-blind. However, they can distinguish many more grey shades between black and white than men. Cats, for example, have an extraordinary sight, mainly at night. At night their eye sight is vastly superior to ours. In the human eye the rods, which distinguish bright and dark, are not that well developed, men are very colour oriented.
Still black and white perception is a very early ability in the evolution of man and is performed by very "old" parts of the human brain. When babies start seeing they first distinguish sharp contrast: light and darkness. Gradually, the child perceives movement and eventually shapes and forms. By the end of the development the child is capable of perceiving colour, i.e. capable of processing the specific colour stimuli and the resulting physiological and psychological reactions.
Hence vision begins with black, white and grey shades. Becher proved (in 1953) that a vegetative plexus runs from the centre region of the retina directly to the mid-brain and the hypophysis causing the hormonal control. The hypophysis, which is a gland in the centre of the brain, is in charge of regulating the inner secretion, i.e. to secrete vitally im-

portant hormones into the blood circulation which control other glands, for example glands that regulate growth.

In terms of colour vision the perception, distinction and reaction to the colour take place in other, newer areas of the brain (in the cerebral cortex/neocortex).

The impact of colours on the main nerve-cords vagus nerve and sympathetic nerve and the few exceptions (colours which are closer connected to the limbic system) were already described in previous chapters.

As far as grey is concerned this means that the "colourless" must be assigned to the primal impressions black and white. However, grey cannot be in the same way equalled to clearly defined polarities, it rather moves between the two poles – neutral, unemotional and empty.

"Grey is neither colourful nor bright, nor dark. It is completely unexcited and clear of any psychical tendency. Grey is neutrality and none of both – neither subject not object, neither inside not outside, neither tension nor release. Grey is not a busy territory but the border par excellence – the border as no-man's-land, the border as outline, as dividing line, as an abstract division in order to organise opposites, "grey is all theory" as an abstraction." (Lüscher)

Dictionaries of etymology (origin of language) list grey as an old Indo-European word (grao, gra, gray) assigning it to terms as "shining" and "shimmering" – not in terms of colour but in terms of texture or consistency (silver).

In terms of symbolism grey is ambivalent. Grey is evasive and remains an unreal shadow, phantasm, phantom, bloodless and joyless. Grey represents the primal calmness as opposed to the axial antithesis purple, the primal movement. Grey is a bipolar colour arbitrating between light and darkness. The grey monotony of everyday life runs smoothly without any ups and downs. Grey can conceal, steady, and block out anything vital. Grey relates to the mental image of old age and bygone eras, like the "grey eminence", for example. Grey is sorrow and misery; grey is the colour of the Nibelungs whose epic ends in the twilight of the gods. In Greek mythology the grey ferryman Charon escorts the souls across the black Acheron into the realm of the shadows (according to Frieling).

Many advanced civilisations like for example Ancient Egypt or China did not know grey as a symbolic colour.

In the astrology grey is assigned to Saturn and the metals lead (dull grey) and silver (shining grey). In proverbs we know a lot of terms using grey to describe hazy matters. The "grey eminence" is an influential politician who remains unknown in the background. The "grey area" is a zone where nothing is clear or definite, for example between legal and illegal. The same goes for the grey market where no usual laws and controls are in place. The "grauer Star" (cataract) describes the opacity that develops in the lens of the human eye and leads to hazy view and even blindness. "Morgengrauen" (dawn) is the name for the diffuse twilight between the dark night ands the upcoming sunlight. The "grey wolves "is a Turkish terror organisation which functions like secret society.

In recent times we know the “grey panthers”, a political party founded by old people in order to fight for their specific interests.
We talk about the “grauer Alltag” describing the drab monotony of the daily routine, we do not want to be a (grey) mouse, i.e. someone insignificant and dull, clouds turn grey when it rains, old and dead wood turns grey, too.
Hence grey has also to do with getting old, paling and dying off. Grey is a very useful colour when used for camouflage but most aspects are negative. People who like grey do not want to reveal their true selves, like in fairy tales they put on the (grey) magic-hood to make their personality invisible, they want to shield themselves from the environment and do not want to “show their colours”.
From tests we know that grey is often used in cases of weariness and fatigue or in situations when people do not want any excitement. Grey is also a favourite colour for exams in order to help concealing the tension (according to Lüscher).
In colour tests which were used as part of personnel selection procedures remarkably many young men all of a sudden chose grey (26,6 % instead of the usual approx. 5%, according to Bokslag).
Children largely reject grey as has been shown many times. The rejection wanes a bit before puberty and gets stronger again at the age of 17, mainly among young women. Men have a greater preference for grey, probably because a grey suit looks relatively inconspicuously in the competitive business day and

therefore does not give any reason to attack the wearer.

However, mostly grey s rejected as boring and dull because of its lack of energy and charisma. People who reject grey associate the colour with fear, in particular fear of getting old and the proximity to death. Darker grey is associated with monotony, depression and hopeless despair.

While a light grey is still perceived as being relatively lightweight, dark grey comes across as comparatively heavy, plenteous and calm. Dark grey is also the colour of dirt. We can say that light grey is a "casual camouflage" – the readiness to respond to stimuli and to react intensely is latent but is being retained because such reactions are considered as inappropriate for the time being.

The same readiness is much more subdued and slowed down in dark grey. Behind this colour hides a hyper sensitive character who longs for a safe and harmonic emotional state and who does not want to be thrown off balance in any way by too strong reactions.

The rejection of both hues reveals states of stasis and may indicate emotional disturbance. Mainly people who reject dark grey suffer from their own sensitivity and decline any emotional bondage because of this suffering.

"Statistic analyses have confirmed that the choice of "colourful" colours and the choice of grey shades come from different areas of the personality because they do not correlate at all. Brightness as simulation of excitement and darkness as calming impression

are possibly closely related to the control of the reticular formation in the brainstem which controls physical behaviours such as sleep. The choice of dark and light therefore may set the tone and characterize the psycho-energetic level of a person." (Lüscher)
If this is true, the preference for or rejection of the specific shade of grey would be a clear indication of the psychical status of stimulation. However, there is more to it. According to Lüscher in a colour test grey always indicates the border line between "permitted" and suppressed emotionality.

Through the grey area the world is divided into a compensatory overestimated and excessive area on the one hand and on the other hand the rest of the world – the possibilities which are devaluated or suppressed by fear. The obvious disproportion between affirmed colours and the carefully suppressed colours is so full of tension that there is certainly a grave conflict behind it.
In the light of colour psychology the "magic-hood" grey does not withstand, the grey camouflage becomes transparent and reveals the emotional state it was supposed to conceal.

The Colour Silver

While gold is an enhanced form of yellow, silver is not an autonomous colour either but the shining form of a greyish white. The precious metal is crystallising, lustrous white, harder than gold, ductile and can take a high degree of polish.

Since ancient times silver has been known as the sister of gold and was always mentioned together with gold. Just like gold it was precious and was frequently used for jewellery, coins and a symbolic colour.

Whereas gold was the shining male colour of the sun and his beneficial impact on earth, the cool, even cold shimmer of silver was assigned to the female principle of the moon and her cyclic impact on life.

In the ancient world human organs were assigned to particular heavenly bodies: the spleen to Saturn, the lungs to Mercury, the gall to Mars and the liver to Jupiter. The organ assigned to the golden sun, however, was the heart and the organ assigned to the silver moon was the brain. We should explain that the brain was not seen as the centre of nerve-cords but rather as the place where associations and equations are located and the stronghold of bygone impressions and the transformation of such impressions into mental images and emotions. Hence it was much more subject to the influence of the moon and her cyclic variations than the “thinking and acting” heart which was assigned to the sun. Silver was therefore a symbolic colour of the matriarchy just like blue, green and in some way black.

The meaning of the word silver which comes from Germanic languages is still unknown. We only know that the silver was already used in the earliest advanced cultures. In Mesopotamia in the 3rd millennium B.C. silver was much more precious and sought-after than gold. The oldest known silver coins come from the times of Hammurabi. The Hethites already owned silver mines and extracted silver from lead ore. Phoenician merchants brought silver from Spain to Egypt where pure silver was unknown; they only knew Electrum, a natural alloy of gold and silver. The imported Phoenician silver was called “the white” and was considered as a specific form of gold.

The Greeks extracted silver in Attica and they called it agyron which means “bright” and “shining”. The Roman word argentums derives from this Greek expression.

Around 100 A.C. Tacitus reported that the Teutons knew silver mining and has smelteries near Wiesbaden and Ems.

The golden age of the German silver mining was the 16th century (for example in Joachimsthal from which name the term “Thaler” for a silver coin was derived). Huge amounts of silver were also found in North America and the Latin Americas as well as Australia.

Since gold was overvalued in the ancient world, silver was allocated the second place in the generally accepted ranking: golden and silver wedding, gold, silver and bronze medals, etc. Perhaps there is a connection between this ranking and the suppression of the matriarchy by the patriarchy. At least we find in many different cultures that the oldest scripts always had the order “silver and gold” while later records switched to “gold and silver”.

The colour psychology does not rate silver (or gold for that matter) as autonomous colours. They do not feature in tests and no special attention is paid to their impression. Much can be said, though, about the frequently used colour in advertising, design, and jewellery design.

The common feature of gold and silver is their ability to shine which attracts so much attention. However silver is not like gold which is clearly oriented to comprehensive warmth, cordiality and the wish to please. Silver is much cooler, more introverted and rational. In contrast to gold silver exercises understatement, controlled restraint as well as restraint of the obvious outward emotionality

Products and packages containing silver convey the impression of high-quality, noble and precious but calmer and quieter as if they rather want to be discovered and conquered than sell out in a loud way. A noble chillness seems to breathe on us, an elegance which has the most distinctive quality when combined with black.

On the whole the deliberate use of gold and silver reflects the ranking of social standards – a deviation from these standards can therefore not be without consequences.

Kaleidoscope of colours

Can you smell, taste and feel colours?

Recently newspapers yet again featured reports about blind people who can “see colour”. The reports were referring to tests which have been carried out very often in researching blindness and which had very surprising results. The tests showed that many blind people have a refined sensitivity which enables them to actually feel out the specific character of various colours with their finger tips.

It’s not really news that the colour spectrum can be divided in so called “cold” and “warm” colours. Goethe already divided his colour circle into two adversely tempered zones. He assigned yellow, orange and red to the warm zone, blue, turquoise and violet to the cold zone. Green has a neutral middle value. Rudolf Steiner’s anthroposophical school, which refers to Goethe’s colour theory, uses these warm/cold characteristics of the colours or certain therapies.

With proceeding differentiation tests (starting with the strongest contrast red-blue and advancing to the mixed colours) the tested blind people succeeded in feeling out the different temperatures of individual colours as Goethe had described them. This is all the more surprising because the test colours are not

physically measurable different wavelengths but actually painted colours i.e. painted or printed pigments which are used for all paintings or magazine photos.
To be honest I have to admit that it is hard for me to comprehend such amazingly outstanding sensitivity. However, I have witnessed myself some cases of blindfolded seeing people who had a very high hit ratio in feeling out warm and cold colours (which was considerably higher than the percentage of random hits). I also know a very successful painter, who is – unbeknownst to the public – colour blind and compensates for his inability to see various colour hues by feeling them out.
The phenomenon of such "indirect vision" has not yet been researched properly. All we can say is that it's a hyper sensitive reaction of the tactile sense that becomes active to make up for the missing vision. However, the well known fact that normal colour perception also always requires the collaboration of multiple senses has been scientifically proven. This collaboration of senses is called synesthesia ("synesthesia" is Greek for "equally sensed"). Synesthesias are parallel perceptions with the collaboration of multiple senses whereas the experts still do not agree if the perceptions are successive (one after another) or simultaneous (at the same time).
The most distinctive features of synthesias are phonisms and photisms. Phonism is a form of synesthesia in which a primary optical signal causes a secondary sensation of hearing either simultaneously or immediately thereafter (e. g. an uttered thought). In terms of colour we speak of "colour hearing".

Photism (also called synopsises), on the other hand, is a synesthesia in which a sensation of colour or light (for example an image that appears in the mind) is caused by an acoustic signal (for example a sudden unexpected noise or spoken word). Vowels, months and names can also be connected to colour experiences.

I think this distinction is rather rough and unsatisfying because in fact not only the senses vision and hearing are involved but also the three others (touching, smelling and tasting) and their numerous combinations. We see how the "zeitgeist" influences such studies by reducing "modern" man to the two distancing senses vision and hearing while the much more intimate emotions of touching, smelling and tasting are not necessarily regarded as essential anymore, at least they are not considered to be worth a thorough scientific study. I have to express my self so explicitly to draw the attention to the background of this development.

While in primitive times men were dependent on the functioning of all senses, when they "tasted their way through nature" on the search for food, when they perceived important and life saving information by smelling and when they had most definitely a very refined sense of touch, they have turned into the "vision and hearing animals" of today. Our sense of smell is very limited – manufacturers of perfume and druggists can tell us a thing or two about it. Our taste is limited as well – we need highly paid experts to evaluate the taste of wine, tea and coffee for us. All gourmets know that the standardized, unimaginative processed food these days also contribute to the loss of our sense of taste. Cigarette smoking adds to the killing of the taste buds. People who quit smoking are amazed when they find after a while how different and intensive their food tastes again. The sense of touch or better: the delicacy of feeling is getting lost more and more as manual work is handed over to machines which only require pushing a button. In a test with high school students only two boys were able to distinguish a marble plate from plastic, polished stone and lacquered wood.

Therefore it comes as no surprise that modern therapies lately have founded so called "sense schools", that performance artists are spectacularly successful when they exhibit "tactual pictures", and that people just shake their heads in disbelief when behaviourists prove that the mass psychological problem panic is initiated by hardly perceivable smelling phenomena and not by optical or acoustical signals – to name just a few examples.

There is a similar preference of senses when it comes to learning these days:

We may perceive our environment with all senses – we hear the thunder, see the lightning, smell the flowers, taste the fruits, and feel things – but the scale of values for learning shows the following percentage:

We learn

through optical information	83.0 %
through acoustic information	11.0 %
through smelling only	3.5 %
through touching	1.5 %
and through tasting only	1.0 %

The values detailed above are responsible for today's common practise to teach subject matter only in a combination of optical and acoustical methods, i.e. audio-visually, in order to get the best learning results. However, creative individuals who use their imagination to create something new should make it their business to avoid the entrenched habit in terms of audio-visual communication, break up the cemented channels of communication and apply themselves to the promotion of the other sensory forces.

Let us return to the starting point of the topic: early on men thought about the mysterious synesthesias. Hence there are numerous interpretations and attempts to describe regularities.

For example – to stay in the context of colours – we know that already in the Middle Ages there were attempts to connect the sound of the language with the character of colours. Common idiomatic expression or popular metaphors are "colour of language", colour hue" and "sound of colour". Music and language – that is to say acoustic areas – have been seen as closely related to the visual world of painting. In the field of literature the rendition of synesthesias and free associations with synesthesias became a characteristic elements of style in the Romantic, the

Symbolism and the Impressionism where they obtained the most beautiful forms of impression (see chapter blue).
The history of combining colour and music can be traced back to L. B. Castel's so called "Colour Organ" which was first used in 1723 and which later inspired many other musicians. The "coloured light music", "colour music" and the "colour-sound art" respectively, were parts of an aesthetic futuristic programme in the times of high baroque and rococo. Mainly in the "romantic programme music" (Liszt, Mussorgski, Reger et al) the idea of combining sound and visuals was put into practice by trying to add sound to paintings. The same quest can be found in animated movies (for example Walt Disney's "Fantasia", see O. Fischinger et al) and occasionally even in feature films (for example Werner Herzog, to name a representative of this genre).
Skrjabin's use of the colour keyboard (1913) in the symphonic poem "Prometheus" picks up the ideas of L.B. Castel. It was played like a piano but projected coloured light on a screen rather than sound. The "light shows" of modern underground and psychedelic music fulfilled the same function – they were designed to make a concert a "total experience". Today similar effects are produced by synthesizers that convert the sound into colour images by means of laser projection which are coupled to the keys which create the sound thus flooding the audience with simultaneous visual-acoustic messages.
There have also been attempts to convert language itself into colour sensation. Each vowel was allocated a

specific colourfulness which corresponded to its point of origin and the depth in the human body of resonance – for example the dark phoneme U corresponded to the dark blue, the even darker O corresponded to an even darker brown, A was assigned to a brilliant, vibrant yellow, I to red, and E to a lighter green in dark environment or a dark yellow (ochre) depending on the accent. (Translator's note: please note that these are German vowels which are pronounced respectively).

If a designer is sensitive enough and if he knows about this archaic colour alphabet, he can convert phonetic language into colour, synchronise it graphically and thus create condensed denotation content.

The "sound painting" provides the student with interesting possibilities to gain experience. For example – dare to try converting abstract terms like "Mulumum", "Zibirr" and "Batata" into colours. Let the magic of the unusual sound construct appeal to you meditatively while you take one colour tube after the other and carry out the first strokes of the brush next to each other. You will find that only certain colours are eligible to convert the terms but others are ruled out from the start. As a side note – you will find that specific shapes come about virtually by themselves in the painting process as the painting stroke changes the rhythm. Certain sounds stipulate an aggressive, rushed brushwork, others lead to rounded undulations, allow only dashing or challenge to do a large scale work. However, do the test yourself without much thinking. Ascending analytical associations will only distract you and may steer the actual creative process into possibly unwanted symbolic links which stand in the way and hamper the free flow of emotion.

Painting to music is another excellent possibility to work freely and to create synchronic connections between acoustics, colour, shape and motion. Accordingly, the meditative way with no intellectual interference is the way that leads into the areas of the archaic colour language deep inside man.

Every experienced designer knows about the importance of such a subliminal conformity of various sensations. No matter if it's the "face" of a company, the design of a package or the supporting resonating of specific colours in an advertising campaign – the good designer "feels" that he uses the identical emotional potential of sender and recipient – mainly when it is not about an individual and self-absorbed design but about mass communication. In a manner of speaking he paints with the colourful protolanguage of mankind which has been acquired and commonly accepted by the cultures over millenniums.

Much lesser known is the fact that touching can trigger a sensation of smelling just like basically all sensory input can be linked.

Psychologists try to explain the still unsolved processes of perception with newly created terms like for example "substitute phenomenon". At this point we can only present an example for such substitute phenomena which cannot do more but aim a single spotlight at a large field which stays largely in the dark. From tests with drug addicts we know that simultaneous perceptions that happened under the influence of drugs generate links which will later create the same effects even without any drug intake. A hashish smoker who listens to a specific kind of music under the influence of the drug, burns some incense sticks, and maybe drinks jasmine tea, can later become just as high without any drugs just by listening to the same music. Maybe he will sense an intensive smell or if he actually burns incense sticks he will suddenly believe to perceive the taste of the jasmine tea which seems to be identical with the mood of the music (or the light).

Using this example we are not saying that "substitute phenomena" and simultaneous perception are only possible under the influence of drugs. Of course, they happen very often in normal state of consciousness as well but they are very rarely recognized unaided.

Many tests have been carried out about the linked meaning of colour and taste, for example in the area food and food packaging. There are very interesting test about coloured food which are preferentially carried out with school kids (years 5/6).

The test is based on the fact that we all have very specific acquired patterns of expectation patterns when it comes to the colours of food. We link a defined taste to the visual perception of a certain colour. If reality is changed by colouring beverages and food with food colours, that is to say colours them in an alienating way, the familiar patterns of expectation get unbalanced and there is virtually no real possibility of derivation.

In our example we work with a plate with uncoloured cookies and three other plates with cookies which are coloured blue, red and green. Of course, at first we will have a discussion about "genuine" and "fake" cookies with a strong rejection of the coloured cookies which are regarded as synthetic and compared to foam, modelling plastic, coloured plasticine and other material. When the first samples are tasted and the taste of the coloured cookies is freely associated, very weird combinations of sensations come about.

The red cookies are all of a sudden sweet as well as acrid and the taste of strawberries, cherries or cherry liqueur is perceived. Strangely, they remind the tested persons more of Christmas than the "normal" yellow cookies which only taste of sugar, butter or lemon and associations are named which are usually typical for the colour red (at this point the observant reader won't be surprised about the fact that the children automatically reached for the red cookies first.)

The green cookies magically obtain a woodruff taste or they taste of flowers and somehow fresh. The blue cookies are suggested to have an acrid aftertaste, although they also taste sweet at first. They are suspected to contain too much gruel, taste of blueberries or rum, maybe even burnt.

Tests with coloured lemonade, which are very easy to carry out, brought similar results (for tests with adults coloured sparkling wine is used, the reactions are the same).

In short, people assign a "natural" taste to their usual food. If the visual impression is different from the

usual one due to colouring or under the influence of coloured light, they immediately start searching for comparisons which fit into the performance repertoire of the colour and invent tastes which are in reality not present in the food.
Another interesting area to get experience with colours is the use of coloured makeup which can turn a face into an angel or a devil. All children enjoy changing into totally different characters by the use of makeup – a characteristic trait that seems to be typically human. The joy of using excessive paint and makeup is acted out in carnival as well as in the theatres by professional artists. Body painting has always been an important cultural, religious and ritual element in many cultures. Think about the traditional definitude of colours in the Japanese theatre, where each actor is defined as a character in his role by minimum use of certain makeup colours. Think also about the war paint and colour painting of the Indians, the ritual body painting in virtually all "primitive" peoples or the use of colours in the early cave paintings which defined specific content by the systematic use of respective colours.
We all know that colours are rarely mute and act by themselves but they are mostly supported by simultaneous sensory input: the painted Indians sing and dance figuratively in a similar way as the dressed up actors do in order to complement and to intensify the desired character impression by adding another sensory level. Even when we buy a packaged food product we invent taste, smell and other qualities triggered by the colour signal.

Our perceived sensory information is linked together so tightly that we often cannot distinguish which message is the more important one – the visual appearance, the acoustic signal, taste, smell or associated haptic experiences. Probably such a separation is not possible and not advisable, either. Basically, the human perception is synesthetic. On our way to a civilised being, we unfortunately lost some of the qualities we used to own initially or we are in danger of forgetting them in favour of a one-sided perception which is almost exclusively limited to the audiovisual element. However, people still have their five senses (not to mention the sixth sense which is located in the borderland of the scientific state of knowledge) – what matters most is that they use them correctly and that means in my opinion they should use them simultaneously and even synchronously.

Healing With Colours

Colours have been used for health treatment since ancient times. The Greek-Roman scholar Galen (Claudius Galenus, 129 -199 A.C.) who worked as the personal physician of the emperor Marc Aurel and whose writings were still highly respected in the late middle ages invented the theory of the four bodily humours. According to the theory the human body is controlled by four fluids: melancholic (black bile), choleric (yellow bile), sanguine (blood), and phlegmatic (phlegm). Depending on the dominating fluid he assigned psychical features and preferences for colours to the respective types of character. : blue to the thick-blooded melancholic, red to the hot-blooded choleric, yellow to the thin-blooded sanguine and green to the cold-blooded phlegmatic – terms and assignments which do not seem to have lost validity up to this day and which look surprisingly up-to-date in the light of modern research.

Since the days of Galen a multitude of scientific studies in the field of medical colour research have been carried out, the most spectacular by Danish physician Niels Ryberg Finsen who introduced the treatment of lupus vulgaris (skin tuberculosis) with concentrated light radiation (blue light), the so called Finsen lamp. 1903 he was awarded the Nobel Price in Medicine for his groundbreaking work about the effects of light and colour. Like Goethe he said that colours are autonomous forces which should not be confused with suggestive power.

Goethe, who valued his "Theory of Colours" higher than his complete poetic work, already wrote: "If you want to feel the singular important effect of a colour to the full, you have to surround the eye completely with this colour, stay in a coloured room or look through a coloured glass. Then you identify yourself with the colour, it attunes eye, spirit and body in unison with itself."

As is well known the Anthroposophists use such coloured rooms for therapeutic purpose. In the anthroposophical hospital in Filderstadt a crimson room and a bright blue room are in use. Patients are asked into the room to either excite them (red) or calm them down (blue) depending on their vegetative state. They say that even blind patients sense these impulses very strongly.

Similar methods are known in psychiatry. In hospitals which provide for the necessary facilities depressive melancholics who are at risk of committing suicide are "retuned" in rooms with red walls, red carpets and red light. Accordingly, raving madmen are calmed down in blue rooms (according to Prof Eberhard). Professor Ponza (Alexandria) healed patients who where in a state of "total refusal", i.e. who refused any intake of food, in yellow sun-drenched rooms. After only one day in such a room the patients began to recover their appetite and started to eat.

Colour therapist Dr. v. Langsdorff found out that red light causes vessels to widen and increases the blood flow whereas blue light narrows the vessels creating a sort of ischemia and making the skin insensitive. These results have been taken up a lot lately. Dentists use blue light for surgery and to avoid toothache.

Furthermore, studies found out that red light treatment has a positive impact on certain skin disease like scarlet fever, measles, and lichen, also colds, hypothermia and frostbites, paralysis, asthma, as well as stagnation in the movement of the heart, lungs and muscles.

Blue light, however, has a noticeable effect on nervous disorders and a yellow light therapy helps healing diseases of the digestive organs (stomach, intestine, liver, kidney, spleen and bladder.) It has been claimed (according to Reichenbach, the discoverer of the "Od rays") that sensitive test persons detect taste differences in water that has been previously exposed to chromatic radiation.

As it often happens in scientific research, these therapies were developed from experiments with plants and animals. Plants which grow under the so called "rays of growth" of red light behave similar to those which live in the dark – they strive to the light faster. Tests with greenhouses made of red glass showed that plants grew four times as fast as in the usual greenhouses.

Blue light, on the other hand, makes plants grow smoothly. However, the more intensive the influence of the blue light becomes, the more effective the "inhibition rays" become. This effect is most intensive in the High Alps where you find a very high natural UV radiation. The plants stay low, develop distinctly smaller leaves and seem to virtually crouch on the ground.

There are similar colour effects on men – wounds heal faster under red light, blue light causes narrow vessels and can therefore be used for the treatment of tumours and goitres etc.

Apparently, people knew about the specific effects of these colours already in early times. In the middle ages they wrapped children who suffered from measles, scarlet fever and other skin diseases into red cloths. This practice is still in use in many primitive tribes today.

People in southern countries seem to know by intuition that the chillness of blue has a repelling impact on insects and in particular flies. They paint their door frames and window frames in the coldest possible colour – turquoise – and combine a cultic symbolic act with a useful measure.

Animal tests with cows, horses, sheep and goats had the same results. Cows in stables which are painted blue yield more milk and have a lot less stress having to chase away flies. Another improvement is achieved by building in yellow windows which give the blue room a greenish gleam reminding the cows of field and grass and quickening their appetite.

Experiments with coloured glass can be reproduced very easily. Spotlight a blindfolded test person standing in a darkroom with different coloured light – if possible let the ray of light touch the person throat right beneath the face. The spontaneous reaction to red light will be that the arms of the person move towards the source of the light while in case of blue light they will move away.

The Indian physician Dr. Ghadiali (Spectro-Chrome-Institute New Jersey) invented a comprehensive colour therapy. He refers to the warm colours red, orange, yellow and yellow-green as the "growth" rays and the cold colours blue, blue-violet and blue-green the "inhibiting" rays and details therapeutic indications for the individual colours:

Blue: is a vitality builder, it brings down fever and feeds the nerves.
Violet: builds spleen, stimulates lymph, and gives energy.
Purple: enhances sexual activities and stimulates veins
Red: builds haemoglobin and supports the senses
Orange: builds lung tissue and stimulates glands
Yellow: strengthens the nerves, promotes digestion and stimulates the stomach
Green-yellow: builds up bones, kills bacteria
Green-blue (turquoise): strengthens the skin

The chrome therapist Wölfle worked with colour light lamps and gave exact instructions for the treatment of individual diseases. In the mean time several colour therapists practice in Germany like for example Schiegl who developed specific irradiation devices, colour activated drugs (colour – organ – complex) and a colour/music therapy (colour – sound –

cassettes) in which he assigned colours to specific sounds:

Red	= Do
Orange	= Re
Yellow	= Mi
Green	= Fa
Blue	= Sol
Violet	= Si

(His scale is based on the old six tone scale)

All these therapies are still at the experimental stage of research and development. It is unfortunate that the fundamental physiological and psychological relevance of colours and their valuable effects still play an outsider role in the field of health treatment and still have no noteworthy influence on the orthodox medicine. In this area we can expect exciting developments and groundbreaking discoveries in the future. However, to make that happen, some disciplines which are currently working independently must finally look beyond the horizon and make the yet untouched zones of interdisciplinary research their field of interest.

Further Studies on Colours

Quick Perception of Colours

The test was performed using a tachistoscope, a device that displays different colours for fractions of a second each. The participants are then asked which colours they perceived first (see Favre and Novembre).

1.	perceived	colour	orange	ca. 21.0 %
2.	"	"	red	ca. 19.0 %
3.	"	"	blue	ca. 17.0 %
4.	"	"	black	ca. 13.0 %
5.	"	"	green	ca. 12.5 %
6.	"	"	yellow	ca. 12.0 %
7.	"	"	violet	ca. 5.5 %
8.	"	"	grey	ca. 0.5 %

In this test the preference for certain colours still plays a role. This explains the relatively high rank of blue and the relatively low rank of yellow.

If we take into account that the results are skewed because of sympathy and antipathy towards the colours and if we take the actual brightness of the colours and their distant effect into account, we get the following corrected result:

1.	best	perceptible	colour:	yellow
2.	"	"	"	orange
3.	"	"	"	red
4.	"	"	"	green

Popularity of Colours

This popularity chart is based on a representative average of the German population and was compiled from various extensive studies by known psychologists (Lüscher, Frieling, Favre, November et al) and test institutes and was confirmed by subsequent field studies:

red
blue
green (beaten by a distance)
yellow (right behind green)
grey
brown
violet
orange (low position although well perceptible)
black
white

Colour Choice by Sick People

According to a study by Prof. Lüscher

green
blue
grey
violet
red
brown
black
yellow

Colour Preferences

Generalised statements about specific groups

Children: all primary colours, rarely mixed colours
Younger people: bright, vivid colours.
Puberty: suddenly rare, problematic colours.
Adults: saturated shining colours, mixed shades of colours.
Older people: dark, weakened colours.
Higher income: pastel shades, colour compositions, graduated colour shades, delicate and pure colours.
Low income: shining, simple colours, also “gaudy” shades.
City: rather colder colours, pastel shades, preference for green and blue.
Countryside: saturated colours, preference for red and patterns.
Brain work: blue
Manual work: red
Introvert: heavy dark colours, mixed colours.
Extroverted: extremely shining colours, full colours.

Colour, Font and Readability

The table below shows which coloured font on coloured background provides for best readability. Karl Borggräfe got the results by using a tachistope to measure the precise reading time. 0.59 inch letters were combined on 3.94 x 9.84 inch planes. The rank:

	font colour	*plane colour*
1	black	yellow
2	yellow	black
3	green	white
4	red	white
5	black	white
6	white	blue
7	blue	yellow
8	blue	white
9	white	black
10	green	yellow
11	black	orange
12	red	yellow
13	orange	black
14	yellow	blue
15	white	green
16	black	red
17	blue	orange
18	yellow	green
19	blue	red
20	yellow	red

Symbolic Allocation of Colours

(According to C. G. Jung)

Colour	***Planet***	***Metal***	***Humour***	***Gender***
Red	Mars	Iron	Choleric	Male
Yellow	Sun	Gold	Sanguine	Male
Green	Moon	Silver	Phlegmatic	Female
Blue	Earth		Melancholic	Female

Astrological Allocation of Colours

Colour	***Planet***	***Characteristics***
Red	Mars	Courage and pugnacity
Yellow	Sun	Majestic dignity and power of life
Green	Venus	Love and joy of love
Blue	Jupiter	Conquest and wisdom
White	Moon	Innocence and devotion
Black	Saturn	Perseverance and depth

Alchemistic Allocation of Colours

Colour	***Metal***	***Planet***	***Organ***
Yellow	Gold	Sun	Heart
White	Silver	Moon	Brain
Blue	Tin	Jupiter	Liver
Green	Copper	Venus	Kidneys
Red	Iron	Mars	Bile
Black	Lead	Saturn	Spleen
Purple	Mercury	Mercury	Lungs

Mystic Allocation of Colours

Colour	***Tarot Cards***	***sign of the Zodiac***	***No.***
Bright red	Magician	Aries	***1***
Green	High Priestess	Taurus	***2***
Blue	Empress	Gemini	***3***
Light violet	Pharaoh	Cancer	***4***
Orange-red	High Priest	Leo	***5***
White	Choice	Virgo	***6***
Indigo-blue	Chariot	Libra	***7***
Dark red	Justice	Scorpio	***8***
Red-violet	Hermit	Capricorn	***9***
Grey	Wheel of Fortune	Sagittarius	***10***
Clear blue	Courage	Aquarius	***11***
Reddish	Hanged Man Ordeal	Pisces	***12***

Conclusion

Man is a creature that orients very strongly by optical signals and learns very intensively through visual messages. Over millenniums man has experienced that colours define the context of the natural environment, has learnt to interpret this context and changed it by civilising intervention. Thus he has a colourful vocabulary at hand which relates to his living conditions, defines importance and serves as a quick orientation guide in everyday life. With progressing cultivation, i.e. conversion of wilderness into civilisation there is a flood of visual stimulation which has made the world more colourful artificially but which therefore also requires more structure and semantics. Within the communication processes clear definitions like colour guidance systems, Corporate Design and psychological colouring of designs take on greater significance. Fashion, advertisement and socially relevant trends sometimes respond to the longing for more individuality and create counter trends which question the usual context of colours we all have learnt and cause visual confusion with a multitude and variety of unusual colouring.
As a result we observe a) a certain fatigue and stupefying which is caused by the flood of stimuli and b) an increasing subconscious acceptance of the "secret" power of the colours.

Many communication processes run quicker than in the past, traditional values have been suspended. The universally valid general consensus of society in previous times has been replaced by target group oriented thinking and acting, a widespread aesthetic insecurity prevails and it is obvious that the sensitivity of many people has decreased.

This is the starting point when we study the current role of colours. An overwhelmingly big majority of more or less passive consumers is faced by a small minority of active "doers". The communication designer has to act as producer of messages and their packages with the main task to establish a clearly understandable unambiguous communication between people. Hereby he uses colours as allocation tool and has therefore to be aware of the psychological impression properties of colours and must know about the possible effects of his designing process. This does not mean that the designer is the "hidden persuader" behind the curtain and is able to manipulate people arbitrarily without limits because of his advantage of knowledge. Much rather he himself is subject to the rules of human colour language when he chooses his techniques. If he does not take the archetypical background, hidden symbolic content and imprints which are dormant in the collective subconscious into account he won't be "fashionable" for long. His success will be superficial and short-lived and his work won't make a lasting impression.

Mainly communication designers must sensitize themselves in order to get the "right feeling" that enables them to use the hidden power of the colours properly, i.e. target oriented and consistently. For example, in my own tutorial I use various creativity training models in order to activate associative thinking and feeling, i.e. I try to promote the interaction between the two brain halves and analyze the resulting feedback. For example I ask: If this product / message were something totally different – a car, a modern sculpture, a dance, music a painting, a house, a landscape – how would it look? Which colouring would be conceivable? Could we apply the same colouring to all examples? I let the students make collages and "impression pictures" to visualise these associations. The effect and significance of individual colours can well be illustrated by black and white photography because superficial colour surfaces are excluded and the essential character of the colour becomes evident – by translating it to another media level.

Whoever plays this game and sees colours as something much more than just refraction of light (physical definition) will soon experience that colours are "visualised feelings". Each colouring has physiological and psychological effects which are so extensive that as a consequence colours can promote health, trigger diseases, they can produce spiritual and emotional harmony or disturbing tension.

Consequently, the designer has a spiritual-aesthetic responsibility way beyond the materialistic view required by the object related task. Dealing with colours is applied psychology and even more – it is also cultural work. The young communication designer, graphic designer and colour designer are not aware of this context at the beginning of their studies and unfortunately advanced students are not aware of it, either. They are in love with their creative activities and want to preserve the area of freedom of creativity, therefore they do not respect (or do not even know about) the experiences other designers made before them. Basically, it is not bad to experiment and to look into the future and to develop the designing process. It's still a pity when designers stop there and do not realise that they can learn the most from reflecting the wealth of experience from the past.

The rock musician who wears yellow glasses in order to "feel good" over a long period of time and who uses the yellow glass as stimulating device, namely a psychological "brightener", probably does not know that Goethe already made the same experiments and passed them on to future generations in almost meditative texts. Therefore, it can be an extraordinary sensual-intellectual joy to re-read his "Theory of Colours" with regard to these aspects and use it as a source to expand our consciousness with its many fresh and astonishingly up-to-date surprises.

This book has no been designed to promote a new "visual school" or to present a scientifically accurate and complete compilation of all possible studies in the fields of colour theory, colour psychology, and colour symbolism. It is rather meant to provide a general survey of the state of affairs for students and interested non-professionals and for all those who have anything to do with colours in the widest sense. For further reading some books are recommended in the bibliography.

Further Reading

Badt, Kurt: Die Farbenlehre van Goghs (Cologne 1981)

Biedermann, Hans: Höhlenkunst der Eiszeit. Wege zur Sinndeutung der ältesten Kunst Europas (Cologne 1984)

Brinker, Helmut: Zen in der Kunst des Malens (Bern/Munich/Vienna 1985)

Bürgi, Bernhard (ed): Rot, Gelb, Blau. Die Primärfarben in der Kunst des 20, Jahrhunderts (Stuttgart 1988)

Cardinaux, H: Verhaltensweise hospitalisierter Kinder (Fribourg 1967)

Chögyam, Ngakpa: Der fünffarbige Regenbogen. Energiearbeit mit der Farb- und Elementsymbolik des tibetischen Tantra, translated from English by Theo Kierdorf and Hildegard Höhr (Freiburg i.Br. 1988)

Dittmann, Lorenz: Farbgestaltung und Farbtheorie in der abendländischen Malerei. Eine Einführung (Darmstadt 1987)

Duerr, Hans Peter: Traumzeit – über die Grenze zwischen Wildnis und Zivilisation (Frankfurt 1983)

Eberhard, Lilli: Heilkräfte der Farben (Munich 1954)

Favre, Jean Paul/November, Andre: Color and communication (Zurich 1979)

Ferguson, Marilyn: Die sanfte Verschwörung – persönliche und gesellschaftliche Transformation im Zeichen des Wassermanns (Basel 1982)
Frieling, Heinrich: Das Gesetz der Farbe (Zurich /Berlin/Frankfurt a.M. 1968)
Frieling, Heinrich: Mensch und Farbe (Munich 1975/1988)
Frieling, Heinrich: Der Frieling-Test. Ein Schnelltest zur Charakter- und Schicksalsdiagnostik (Marquartstein no year)
Fromm, Erich: Anatomie der menschlichen Destruktivität (Reinbek near Hamburg 1977)
Gage, John: Kulturgeschichte der Farbe. Von der Antike bis zur Gegenwart. Translated from English by Magda Moses and Bram Opstelten (Ravensburg 1994)
Gericke, Lothar/Schöne, Klaus: Das Phänomen Farbe. Zur Geschichte und Theorie ihrer Anwendung (Berlin 1773)
Goethe, Johann Wolfgang: Zur Farbenlehre. Didaktischer Teil und Polemischer Teil, in: Goethes Werke Weimar edition) Pt. 2 vol. 2 (Weimar 1890) reprint Munich 1987
Gross, Rudolf: Warum die Liebe rot ist (Düsseldorf /Vienna 1981)
Heimendahl, Eckart: Licht und Farbe. Ordnung und Funktion der Farbwelt (Berlin 1961)
Heller, Eva: Wie Farben wirken (Reinbek 1989)
Itten, Johannes: Kunst der Farbe. (Ravensburg 1881)
Knuf, Joachim: Unsere Welt der Farben. Symbole zwischen Natur und Kultur (Cologne 1988)

Langgsdorf, Georg v.: Die Lichtstrahlen (Wiesbaden 1900)
Lüscher, Max: Psychologie der Farben (Basel 1969)
Lüscher, Max: Der Lüscher-Test (Reinbek 1971)
Lüscher, Max: Der 4-Farben-Mensch (Munich 1977)
Matisse, Henri: Farbe und Gleichnis. Collected Writings, translated by Sonja Marjasch (Frankfurt a.M. /Hamburg 1960)
Pawlik, Johannes: Theorie der Farbe. Eine Einführung in begriffliche Gebiete der ästhetischen Farbenlehre (Cologne 1979)
Pötzl, Otto: Über die Beziehungen des Großhirns zur Farbenwelt (Vienna/Bonn/Bern 1958)
Riedel, Ingrid: Farben in Religion, Gesellschaft, Kunst und Psychotherapie (Stuttgart 1990)
Schiegl, Heinz: Color-Therapie (Freiburg i.Br. 1979)
Schöne, Albrecht: Goethes Farbentheologie (Munich 1987)
Steiner, Rudolf: Das Wesen der Farbe (Dornach 1980)
Vogt, Hans Heinrich: Farben und ihre Geschichte. Von der Höhlenmalerei zur Farbchemie (Stuttgart 1973)
Zwimpfer, Moritz: Farbe – Licht, Sehen, Empfinden. Eine elementare Farbenlehre in Bildern (Bern/Stuttgart 1985)

The Author

Harald Braem, born in Berlin in 1944.
Studies: visual communication, psychology and marketing. Worked with Young & Rubicam in the "purple Milka cow" team; worked with Compton/Saatchi & Saatchi as a creative director and head of international marketing campaigns.
Professor of colour theory and colour psychology at the University of Applied Sciences in Wiesbaden from 1981 to 2000. Member of the expert team in the Federal Association of German psychologists. Lecturer at the Gutshof-akademie Frielendorf.
Braem contributed to numerous radio and television programmes on the subject (for example Terra X „Die Magie der Farben“, 2015, ZDF).
In 2005 the documentary „Farbpsychologie. Entdecken Sie Ihre Wohlfühlumgebung“ (coloury psychology – discover your feel-good setting) by Rainer Wälde won the prestigious World Media Award.

For more information see:
www.haraldbraem.de
https://www.gutshof-akademie.de/akademie/ausbildung/ausbildung-wohnberater-einrichtungsberater/
https://www.elvea-shop.de/advanced_search_result.php?categories_id=0&keywords=harald+braem&inc_subcat=1
https://shop.spreadshirt.de/harald-braem/

Die abenteuerlichen Reisen des Juan G.
ISBN: 978-3-946751-88-5

Gilgamesch – Band 1 – Der Löwe von Uruk
ISBN: 978-3-946751-90-8

Gilgamesch – Band 2 – Reise zum Licht
ISBN: 978-3-946751-91-5

Die Wälder meiner Kindheit
ISBN: 978-3-946751-92-2

Atlantis-Botschaft
ISBN: 978-3-946751-94-6

www.ingramcontent.com/pod-product-compliance
Ingram Content Group UK Ltd.
Pitfield, Milton Keynes, MK11 3LW, UK
UKHW062253290726
14090UKWH00017B/669